A different ga<u>me</u>

A different game

HERSHEL SARBIN AND JIM BROWN

golf after 50

Illustrations by Marty Bee

BURFORD BOOKS

IN FOND MEMORY OF EDDIE LEWIS, good friend and colleague whose enthusiasm for the game of golf was always in harmony with his joy of life. Founder of International Golf Safaris with his wife Dorothy, he was a true original in blending the pleasures of golf, travel, and just plain companionship.

10 9 8 7 6 5 4 3 2 1

Library of Congress Cataloging-in-Publication Data
Sarbin, Hershel.
    A different game: golf after 50/ Hershel Sarbin and Jim Brown;
    illustrations by Marty Bee.
        p. cm.
    Includes index.
    ISBN 1-58080-095-5
    1. Golf for the aged. I. Title: Golf after 50. II. Brown, Jim, 1940- III. Title.
GV966.5 .S37 2001
796.352—dc21

                                                  200143279

acknowledgments

FROM THE BEGINNING, *A Different Game* required the unselfish assistance of teaching professionals, tour players, fitness specialists, nutritionists, physicians, psychologists, spouses, and most of all, Golf After 50 readers. For more than two years we have received comments, questions, tips, stories, and story ideas from the very people for whom Golf After 50 was being written. Our names are on the cover, but we consider these golfers to be partners and collaborators.

With absolute certainty that we will omit the name of someone who should have been included, here are some of the people who deserve particular recognition.

Bill Black and Brian Henley, two single-digit golfers, for their six-digit counsel and encouragement.

Bill Binenstock, director of production at CBS Sportsline.com, who, as managing editor of GolfWeb.com, made the decision that Golf After 50 had value for his readers. Always accessible, always contributing, never too busy to pay personal attention to his authors, Bill and production manager Joe Flynn deserve much more credit than these words convey.

Sandy Mills, who, among her other day-to-day tasks, has managed the constant flow of information from New York to Georgia to Florida to New Jersey, and around the world.

Annette Webb, Brian Gleeson, Amelia Bellows, and Marty Bee for their continuing creative and artistic contributions.

Our friend Dick Altman, a longtime associate and public relations counsel, for his early help in crafting copy that captures the spirit of the after-50 golfer.

Tony Chateauvert, Mike Perpich, Judith Roer, Rick Martino, Butch Baird, and Billy Casper, among the scores of teaching and touring professionals who provided reader-friendly technical advice.

Peter Burford and his staff at Burford Books, who made writing, editing, designing, publishing, and promoting the book interesting, enjoyable, and exciting.

Finally, we thank Susan Sarbin and Arlene Brown. With just a word, a question, a glance, or the absence of any response at all, they patiently and enthusiastically made contributions as valuable as anyone already mentioned.

—Hershel Sarbin and Jim Brown

contents

2 Best-Ever Tips

3 Older and Stronger

4 To Your Health

5 Where Does It Hurt?

6 The Back Nine

preface

GOLF AFTER 50, plus or minus a few years, is a different game. It's not the golf we played 10, 20, or 30 years ago. It's not Tiger Woods or David Duval golf. It's not even the game played on the Senior PGA Tour. At 50, 60, 70, experience becomes more important as mentor and guide. Shot selection and accuracy replace power. *Play smart* becomes the golden rule of senior golf. Moreover, what you eat affects what you shoot. How you take care of your body has an impact on your game—and your life. The way you swing a club today determines whether you can swing at all tomorrow, next week, or next year.

I have lived through the agony that accompanies changes in aging bone and muscle and afflicts the long-ago, all-around athlete I thought inhabited my body. "Never give in! Play through pain! Ride that bike! Hit that leg press!" I've done it all and I was not the first to understand that, at least after 60, I could not re-create the body I once knew.

In 1999 I was invited to establish a Golf After 50 Web page on CBS Sportsline.com and PGATour.com. I recruited Jim Brown, editor of the *Georgia Tech Sports Medicine and Performance Newsletter,* as collaborator and coauthor.

a different game   **11**

We set out to provide commonsense advice for people who want to "stay the course" and enjoy it. We've sifted, lifted, listened, and incorporated the advice of professional golfers, physical therapists, nutritionists, orthopedists, and readers willing to share their hands-on experience. Our twice-a-month column deals with the joys and trials experienced by those of us who are making the adjustment from that youthful game we once played to something more senior.

When Jim writes, I edit. When I write, Jim edits. We talk, e-mail, reshape, and refresh. Is it easy? Does it just fly off the keyboard? No. Economy of language—brevity with meaning—is in my experience never accomplished casually.

We are very proud of the illustrations by Marty Bee, a talented original from Louisiana. His spirit is sprightly and his good-natured drawings support our thesis that golf is indeed a good walk.

In the department of friendly counsel, 97-year-old Turkey Righter, a neighbor, holds a special place. His "Modified Rules of Golf"—also known as Turkey's Rules of Enjoyment—and some reader responses are set forth in section 6.

Another personal decision was to keep our coverage and commentary on golf travel quite brief, simply because travel has little to do with golf being "a different game" before or after 50. We seniors may have additional time to travel for the purpose of playing golf, or we may play casually while traveling. But the sensory experience has little to do with age. We have, on our Web site, referenced what we think of as the Best of Golf Travel Articles. But to use the travel vernacular, it's simply not a destination we chose for this trip.

Our great hope is that you'll have an easy journey through our pages. We will be rewarded fully, in fact, if you nod in good-natured agreement as you read, or occasionally roll your eyes in disbelief, or are moved to think about an approach you've never considered. We want you to score better, feel better, and enjoy the game even more than you did when reaching the green in regulation was part of your everyday expectation.

Finally, we look always for new ideas, new expressions, new experiences from you. This book is not the end of the story. The column continues, the learning experience continues, the joy continues, made all the better when we hear from you. So keep going to www.pgatour.com/practice (also reachable by going to www.cbs.sportsline.com—then selecting PGA Tour, practice tee, instruction, golf after 50).

We'll be there looking for you, and listening as well.

—Hershel Sarbin

1 swinging, not swaying

There are very few perfect swings on the Senior PGA Tour, much less among those of us who play golf for fun and exercise. Even golfers with great swings lose them occasionally. In this section you'll find expert advice from teaching professionals, physicians, after-50 golfers, and exercise scientists on how to swing a club in ways that will take strokes off while adding years. This section is about shots you used to hit, shots you shouldn't hit, and what to do when your strokes begin to fall apart. There are discussions of compact swings and connected swings, taped swings, swinging without swaying, winterproofing your swing, and swinging with a bad back. Finally, get ready for your next round with a 10-minute warm-up that works for golfers of all ages.

Single-Digit Memory

"I used to be a 5 and now I'm a 20," an after-50 golfer tells his pro. "I'm retiring now and I'd like to get my handicap below 10 again."

"Lots of golfers over the age of 50 have single-digit memory," says Rick Martino, director of instruction for the PGA of America. "They remember when they had a single-digit handicap, but they don't take into account the fact that things have changed and that a 5 handicap may not be a realistic goal without total dedication to the game."

Martino, who also provides golf commentary for TNT Sports, says that older golfers can, however, reduce their handicaps by getting individualized instruction tailored to bodies that have changed. "The first thing we should do is get into a golf-specific exercise program. Most of us won't stick to a general conditioning program, but an improved golf score is a great motivator that may make us stay with a routine directly related to the game."

Martino is a great believer in what he calls swing fan tools. "They are clublike tools that provide constant resistance without being weighted. The air resistance can help build strength, and that can lead to faster club speed. Remember that we lose some of our fast-twitch muscle capability as we get older; we have to work to get it back. Fast-twitch muscle fibers are the ones that allow us to make quick, forceful movements. It's never too late to improve. I've seen players in their 90s gain strength."

A SWING THAT FITS

"The second thing (after prescribing a golf-specific exercise program) a good teaching professional should do with an after-50 student," says Martino, "is help the student develop a swing that fits his or her body. Very few of us are as flexible as we used to be, so we should not play from an open stance or any other stance that causes right-handers to hit to the left. An open stance restricts the amount of turn possible in the torso and forces us to use our arms more than we should."

Martino says that a slightly closed stance is preferable—one that encourages a hook or draw and will add 15 to 20 yards on some shots. Being parallel to the ground with the shaft at the top of the swing should not be a goal. The goal is for the backswing to end at the point where flexibility also ends. Stay away from a pre-conceived notion of where your backswing should be.

ROUTINES

"Develop a preshot and in-shot routine," advises Martino. "This is something seniors tend not to do. Part of that routine, for example, should be to focus on an intermediate target instead of a long-distance spot. Our eyes are not as good as they used to be. Pick a target somewhere between the ball and the ultimate target."

Things That Go Wrong

A hundred things can go wrong with a golf swing, and any one of them can cause a mis-hit. We all know it, and the misses seem to become more frequent as we grow older. Muscle memory seems to go before the mind does.

Meanwhile, we're all lucky to be walking, swinging, remembering, and talking about our games. Ready or not, here is a short list of things that can go wrong:

✓ Not getting set before the swing.

✓ Losing that soft touch during the swing.

✓ Moving the club too fast during the swing.

✓ Forgetting "turn–turn" (turn away from the ball, then turn back).

✓ Head movement, even peeking.

✓ Coming out of the swing (getting out of the swing plane by allowing the left shoulder to rise too early).

✓ Over the top (forcing your wrists to rotate or turn instead of letting them follow the natural movement created by your body).

✓ Sliding, not turning (shifting your weight from front to back to front rather than rotating your hips and trunk).

That's a quick take on what can go wrong. A friend said, "Golf is a game of misses." He thought he was quoting Gene Littler, but it doesn't matter. It makes sense.

CHATEAUVERT'S LIST

Teaching professional Tony Chateauvert of Bedford, New York, has his own short list of swing thoughts, and they emphasize things to do instead of things to avoid. They include aiming the club face (leading edge) to the target, looking down the target line, and swinging toward the target. The most important thing Chateauvert does as a teacher is remember what each student is capable of doing.

Compact and Connected

"It's never too late to be awesome," says Judith Roer, a Class A LPGA teaching professional at the Boulders Resort in Carefree, Arizona. And Roer has a solid base on which she rebuilds games and sets after-50 players on a path toward becoming awesome.

"As we get older, we tend to lose flexibility and upper-body strength, but we also become lax in our posture," explains Roer, a former touring professional. "The core of any great golf swing is the address position. So I zero in on my students' posture in addressing the ball and try to get them into balance. I want them to work from the hips instead of bending over at the waist. I also teach a narrow triangle formed by both arms off the front of the chest instead of a wider or longer triangle that would be formed by fully extended arms held away from the body.

"Then I try to get them to build their swings from the ground up," she continues. "The motion is more compact and connected, using bigger muscles from the core of the body instead of just the arms. The muscles, whether big or small, should complement each other.

"The balance factor (on both the backswing and the follow-through) gives more power and distance than a swing that uses just the small muscles of the shoulders, arms, and hands. Some players discover power that they never knew they had. Losing flexibility may limit the degree of rotation, but a balanced and symmetrical rotation will result in maximum power and control of the ball's flight."

What's the hardest point about this approach to get across to over-50 golfers? "What they interpret as a more restricted swing is actually torque being created. I try to educate them about a swing that feels compact and connected. If it feels too loose and free, it's usually because the arms are doing all the work."

BUILDING FROM THE GROUND UP

Roer has more to say about building a swing from the ground up. "Once players understand the difference between a compact, connected swing and a swing in which the arms do too much of the work, they fall in love with the idea," says Roer. "It feels effortless. With the arms-only swing, they are more likely to mention neck pain, back pain, shoulder problems, tennis elbow, and so on. A lot of the ailments fly right out of the window because the torso is now actually absorbing much of the shock."

How long does it take a typical golfer to make the switch to the more compact swing? "Usually, they can get the idea, make the change, and see the difference within an hour. It does not take thousands of balls, but rather an understanding about creating a new approach."

Roer calls it an "in-body experience," working from inside the circle out and letting the club become an extension of your compact motion. The opposite of this approach would be starting at the ball and club and working in. She wants players to manage motion instead of just hitting the ball.

Warns Roer, "There should be a slight pause on the backswing. It's vital to allow the big muscles of the trunk to start the rotation. This pause is more like a nanosecond than a pronounced delay. It's like taking a car from reverse to drive. You don't do it all at one time or you'll strip the transmission.

"The finish of the swing should be in symmetry with the back-swing, both in the degree of rotation and in the mind's eye," she adds. "If I rotate three-quarters to the right, then I should finish with a three-quarter rotation to the left and hold the position.

"Most people never attain the finish position," she concludes. "They feel the ball and quit. Their weight is still on the back foot, the ball goes to the right, and they wonder why they don't have any power. It's because the body stops."

Cut Strokes: Tee Off Later

"The older I get, the longer it takes for my body to loosen up," says Don Brown, 65, a 10-handicapper from Dallas. Brown's solution is to delay his tee time until noon or later.

"If I tee off at noon or later, my game is 4 strokes better than if I tee off earlier. Golf is all about getting into a rhythm, and I can get into that zone a lot better when I tee off later. I'm more erratic in the morning. I might play a good hole, then follow it with a triple bogey. I normally shoot in the mid-80s, but after midday I consistently score in the 78 to 82 range. The four par rounds I've shot were all in the afternoon."

Adds Brown, "I've gotten to the point where I negotiate the tee time when I play against my son, Steve. He wants to get out there early. I'm trying to make up reasons why we should start later."

A SCIENTIFIC EXPLANATION?

Is Brown on to something here? Probably. Dr. Edmund Burke, a leading exercise scientist, confirms that hormone levels, body temperature, and muscle flexibility are all at their peak later in the day. All these factors should have a positive effect on athletic performance.

If you have the option of starting your rounds at different times during the day, compare the scores you post. Check past scorecards to see if there's a connection. You may be 4 shots better than you think you are.

A Billy Casper Putting Lesson

"I came up to the 18th in the Bob Hope Desert Classic in the late 1960s, watched Palmer birdie the hole, and knew I had to do the same to win the tournament," remembers Billy Casper, one of the great putters in golf history. "I hit a 4-wood into the center of the green, about 35 feet from the pin. I putted to within about 3 feet of the hole and tapped it in. As I walked off the green, General Eisenhower congratulated me and said that that last putt must have been a real knee-knocker. But it was a putt I had practiced a lot, and when the situated presented itself, I just took care of business.

"Two years later," continues Casper, "I had to sink a 3-footer to win the Carling World Championship in a playoff against Al Geiberger. A miss would have cost me about $18,000—$6,000 a foot. My knees started knocking and I had to walk away. I came back and holed the putt, but it wasn't until then that I really experienced what Eisenhower was talking about.

PRACTICING SHORT PUTTS

"Most of us get a little twitchy on short putts as we get older, so we have to work harder to maintain our putting stroke," he continues. "We ought to spend two-thirds of our practice time on short putts (3 feet and less) and one-third on long putts. When I practice, I imagine putting the ball into that 3-foot circle surrounding the hole.

"The key is to position yourself the same way each time, whether it's a right- or left-breaking putt. Hit the putt on the same place on the putter whether the shot is uphill or down. Then you just have to worry about regulating the force that you use. Keep your eyes and head still and focus on the back of the ball. That keeps you from looking up. Use a smooth, unhurried stroke and try to keep the putter low to the ground on the backswing."

OFF-GREEN PUTTING

Casper uses the putter at times when he's not on the green. "I used to watch Jack Burke use a putter from 20 or 30 feet off the green and couldn't understand why he did it. Now I know why. If you use a club that gives the ball loft, you have to worry about how high and how far to hit it. With the putter, you know you're going to hit the ball right. All you have to worry about is distance. The putter is the easiest club to use. It's not as spectacular, but it saves strokes and that's what the game is about."

Old Dogs, New Tricks

People in our age group know there are some things that our bodies simply can't do anymore. It has nothing to do with determination or willingness to change. Age takes a toll. If it didn't, all those players on the Senior PGA Tour would still be playing on the regular tour.

But that doesn't mean every over-50 player and every teaching professional has to give in to each problem associated with aging. Mike Perpich, director of instruction at RiverPines Golf in Atlanta, is one of those people.

PERPICH DOESN'T BUY IT

"I don't accept the idea that old dogs can't learn new tricks," says Perpich. "A lot of golf instructors just try to pacify students in the over-50 age group. I approach a lesson with these two thoughts: First, that each person is going to get the best instruction possible, regardless of age. And second, that the ball doesn't know how old you are."

Perpich, who has worked with tour players Frank Nobilo and Grant Waite, says that the responsibility for getting good instruction also lies with the person taking the lesson. "Even though some older golfers sign up for lessons," he continues, "they have mental barriers that they can't learn something new. I don't let them get away with that stuff. If they tell me they've been doing something that's wrong for 50 years, I tell them that it's no good; they're going to have to change. In the long run, the over-50 crowd will respond to that approach with respect, and the pro will probably have a customer for life."

The Atlanta teaching pro also believes in tackling mental and physical problems head-on. He thinks golf pros should develop personal relationships with their students to better help them overcome problems brought on by age or injury. "If a player is so inflexible that he or she can't bend down to put a ball on a tee," thinks Perpich, "we have to find out why. A stretching program, a walking routine, or a change in eating habits may solve as many problems as correcting a swing. But you have to know the person well enough to ask personal questions.

"If the problem is a physical condition that can't be changed, my job is to work with the player to minimize the problem. Both of us have to put something into the learning process if it's going to work."

Perpich concludes, "No one has mastered this game and no one will. One of the fun parts of golf is having a game plan as well as a plan to improve. Everyone can get better, even if it means changing something that you've been doing forever or overcoming a problem that seemed insurmountable."

Learning New Skills

Changing the way we drive, chip, pitch, or putt takes more time than most of us after-50 golfers want to commit. Professional golfers put in as much as two months of daily practice before using something new in tournament play. Recreational athletes may need more than this, but we also have the luxury of experimenting in low-pressure competition.

The first step is to get a teaching professional or friend who has mastered the skill to work with you on breaking it down into component parts. Someone who can see only the big picture is of little help. A skilled player or teacher can see if all the parts are in the right place, instead of just seeing where the ball goes.

The second step is one many senior golfers skip, either because they aren't comfortable with the idea or because they don't believe it will work. But there's plenty of evidence to show that it does work. Try to visualize yourself hitting the shot and executing the new skill. You can do this at home, in the car, on the course, or anywhere else when you have a few moments. Next, go through the motions by yourself. It may look a little strange to your friends, but it doesn't have to be much different from taking practice strokes before a shot.

The third step is to work on the new skill during real but unimportant play. Find an opportunity to experiment when little or nothing is at stake. When you're taking the time to develop something new, you have to be willing to hit a bad shot or lose to a lesser opponent.

Finally, develop enough confidence to make the new skill an automatic response in pressure or tournament situations. If you have to think first about trying it, your new toy is not ready for prime time. At this stage, the goal is not to analyze, plan, or experiment. Just do it.

Equipment Adjustments

Almost everything else about golf is different after the age of 50, so it should come as no surprise that some of the clubs in our bags should be different also.

Listen to Senior PGA Tour member Butch Baird. "As we get older, our club speed gets slower. To compensate for that loss, get some 5-, 7-, and 9-woods into your bag. You'll get the same distance you would have gotten with an iron, plus more height, and the ball will stop a lot quicker. Also, look for drivers and irons with a little more flex than traditional clubs."

Billy Casper agrees with Baird on the club-flexibility issue. "We don't have the club speed we once had. Look for drivers and irons with a little more flex—which will give a bit more speed. Don't be stubborn about this. Fit the clubs with what you can do, not with what you think or wish you can do."

Chris McSpadden, head pro at TPC at Sugarloaf, pleads with senior golfers to take advantage of the new technology on the market. "Try graphite shafts, extra-light shafts, titanium heads, and more forgiving heads. In general, seniors ought to use drivers that are lighter and longer."

Master PGA professional Tom Losinger adds his thoughts on the subject of club length. "Seniors tend to play with clubs that are too short. If they don't work on flexibility, they get tight in the hamstrings and can't keep the posture necessary for a comfortable swing. One solution is to use drivers and irons that are longer so they can set up taller and not have to bend over so much. With longer clubs, it's easier to maintain their posture throughout the swing, including the follow-through.

"Also," continues Losinger, "seniors don't seem to get enough loft on their shots. They try to make up for the low trajectory by hitting off the back foot. They'd be better off with 2- or 3-woods off the tee. That would give them the missing loft and make them less likely to compensate in a way that affects the whole swing."

Billy Casper gets the final word on—what else?—putters. "My belief is that most of the greens on today's courses are so good, it makes sense to use a putter that lets you lock yourself into a putting line. Long putters do that. If you can get the blade of the putter on that line, the rest is pretty simple. I have a friend in the Washington area, Bobby Morris, who uses a long putter and rarely has 30 putts per round. Before you make the switch, I recommend that you first spend a little time working with a teaching professional or friend who has experience using long putters."

All these professionals are telling us the same thing: It may be time to reevaluate our weapons. That means at least considering fewer long irons and more 5-, 7-, and 9-woods; lighter, longer, flexible, and high-tech shafts; and long putters. Don't change everything overnight, but gradually start using clubs that add distance and let you maintain control.

Let's Go to the Videotape

Teaching isn't just a matter of listening and remembering. What the student is capable of doing isn't just a matter of making some adjustments for what we'll call the "limitations of age." It also includes trying to figure out how the student's memory system works and how to provide postlesson guidance.

Here's a great example. After a lesson, most of us try our best to remember what we were told whenever we go out to practice or play. Sometimes the pro makes a videotape of the session and then, back in the pro shop, shows us what we did right and wrong. But the trick that works for us is to take home our own video and watch the 5 or 10 minutes of what we did right—*not* what we did wrong—before going out to play the next time.

In fact, we've now started stretching while watching the video. We've also begun doing stretches that mirror some of the movements we take during our swings. This works, too, and we're kicking ourselves less as the process moves along.

Senior Sway

Senior sway is not a new dance step, but rather a bad habit that many after-50 players develop.

Guest pro Mike Perpich, head teaching professional at RiverPines Golf in Atlanta, describes senior sway in right-handed golfers as leaning the body to the right, away from a direct line with the ball. "But in the past few years," he adds, "golfers have been bombarded with the term *turn,* which has resulted in many golfers becoming twisting machines. They're twisting the upper body over the lower body. In the process, how the club shaft, arms, and hands should get in sync with the pivot of the shoulders has been ignored. The bottom line is that many golfers really don't sway. They twist."

Perpich has an answer to the problem: "The solution is to learn a proper pivot, which means rotating around a center point. Try this drill. Stand erect and place a golf shaft across the front of your chest, crossing your arms to hold the shaft against your shoulders. Start at a point out in front of your eye line to the ball and allow your shoulders to rotate 90 degrees to the right. Keep your lower body quiet and let it react to the pivot. Once your shoulders are back, pivot them forward to where you started and continue the pivot to the left 90 degrees. Allow the back (right) foot to finish the movement on your toes. Let your head and eyes rotate to the left and follow the flight of the ball. Don't worry about keeping your head still. That's a completely different subject."

TRUE PIVOT

A true pivot allows you to use the power of your feet and legs properly. Perpich never uses the term *weight shift*, because it implies a side-to-side movement. He teaches that a golf swing is all about a circle, not a straight line. *Sway* is an overused term associated with a bad pivot.

"If you can work on the pivot," he concludes, "you'll create balance and power you don't realize you have, regardless of your age. Throw away the word *sway*. If your body doesn't seem to be working as it should, you're probably twisting (not swaying) instead of pivoting."

Not Touchy, Not Feely

We went back to teaching pro Mike Perpich to ask about *great touch* and *soft hands,* terms we hear in TV commentary. Perpich thinks they're more popular expressions than descriptions of what should happen with the short game between the hands and the club.

TOUCH IS OVERRATED

"Touch is overrated," he claims. "The only responsibility I give the hands during a swing is to hold the golf club. I carry a writing pen with me when I teach and use it to illustrate that you don't have to squeeze it to write with it. Just hold on to it with the thumb, index finger, and middle finger and let the other muscles and motions make the pen move.

"Same thing with the golf club," Perpich continues. "The pressure between your fingers and the club should be constant from beginning to end. There's no reason to squeeze harder on some shots than on others. Just get the right grip and hold on."

Perpich isn't finished. "Most (right-handed) after-50 players were taught to hold the club diagonally in the left hand with too much of the palm holding the club. If you don't hold it in your fingers, the club can't be cocked up. When you hold the club in the palm of your left hand and too high in your right hand, you end up

rolling your wrists. Without the cocking position, you can't get the ball up in the air. The reason Tiger Woods can hit those flop shots around the green is because of the cocked position of his wrists.

GRIP BEATS HANDS

"One more thing about the wrists," says Perpich. "They should work in only one direction—up and down, cocked or uncocked, either toward your face or away from it. They shouldn't be bending toward the left or right of your body. Getting a good grip, not sensitive hands, is what allows you to have great touch and feel around the greens."

You may not agree with Perpich, but he does make you think about the mechanics of "touch" shots.

A Swing for Bad Backs

The combination of advancing age and the cumulative effect of thousands of golf shots has placed those of us in the golf-after-50 crowd in the high-risk group for low-back pain. But help is on the way.

Charles Sorrell, a teaching professional at Golf Meadows in Stockbridge, Georgia, has gained a reputation as the golf pro for players with bad backs. He teaches a golf swing that fits each person's needs, but there are some common denominators in his methods that are working for golfers who might not have been able to continue without his help.

ARMS FIRST

"People who have back injuries," explains Sorrell, "have heard a lot about the importance of body motion in the swing. But we prefer those who are over 50 to allow their arms to swing, and to let their bodies respond to that motion. I'm not talking generating power with your arms only, but letting the body move with them. Most teaching pros place a heavy emphasis on winding or coiling the body, but most after-50 golfers don't have enough flexibility to wind up into anything.

"We encourage letting the left heel lift off the turf on the backswing. That doesn't mean consciously lifting the heel, but rather allowing it to be lifted by the motion. At the same time, we recognize that the head will respond to the winding motion of the shoulders. It moves slightly back as the club begins to move back."

Sorrell says that when you're swinging this way, you shouldn't feel any tension as the backswing is completed, even if you have a bad back. "At the top of the backswing, you should be relaxed and able to flex your right knee. You have to have some flexibility, but not as much as younger golfers. Don't be afraid to allow your hips to rotate somewhat on the backswing."

DON'T BRUISE THE APPLE

The drill Sorrell uses to teach this motion is called Don't Bruise the Apple. He puts an apple in the bottom of a sock and asks his students to swing the weighted sock like a club. If the backswing is correct, the end of the sock with the apple in it touches softly between the shoulder blades. On the follow-through, the apple-in-the-sock again comes in for a soft landing at the same place.

"It's a wonderful drill to teach senior golfers timing and rhythm. It gets them out of the thought of moving the arms with the body—instead, letting the body react to the movement of the arms," adds Sorrell. "If you're an average senior golfer in reasonably good health, you should carry the ball 220 to 225 yards off the tee."

The 10-Minute Warm-Up

Orthopedic surgeons tell us that it would take 45 minutes to warm up all the muscles and joints we need to get us through 18 holes of golf. But that's not going to happen. Most of us are going to squeeze an abbreviated, unscientific warm-up into the few minutes before we tee off.

Dr. Timothy Hosea, an orthopedic surgeon and professor at the Robert Wood Medical School in New Brunswick, New Jersey, has designed the following 10-minute warm-up that is a reasonable compromise for the over-50 golfer. We put this into the category: "You may have heard it before, but this time give your body, and your game, a break. Do it."

STRETCHING

(TWO MINUTES, FIVE STRETCHES, 20 SECONDS EACH)

✓ **Neck Rotations:** Slowly roll your neck clockwise and counterclockwise.

✓ **Shoulder Stretch:** Hold a golf club with both hands and raise it over your head. Place the club behind your back, extend your shoulders upward, and hold. Then, without the club, grasp one elbow and stretch your shoulder by pulling the elbow across the back of your body. Do the same with the other elbow.

✓ **Trunk Side Bends:** With your hands on your hips, bend side to side.

✓ **Trunk Rotation:** Assume the position in which you address the ball, but with your arms across your chest and your hands resting on opposite shoulders. Rotate the shoulders (not the hips) and hold in each direction.

✓ **Toe Touches:** Standing erect, bend forward from the waist and try to touch your toes. If you can't, go as far as you can without hurting yourself, or bend your knees slightly. Hold the position, then slowly stand up. If you have a bad back, do this exercise sitting on a bench and leaning forward.

DRIVING-RANGE PRACTICE (THREE MINUTES)

Hit shots with a pitching wedge, 5-iron, and driver, spending a minute with each club. Use a half swing with the wedge, a three-quarter swing with the 5-iron, and a full swing with the driver.

PUTTING (FOUR MINUTES)

Spend two minutes putting back and forth across the green, getting the feel of the green. Then, for two minutes, practice straight and breaking 3-foot putts.

WAITING TO TEE OFF (ONE MINUTE)

Spend 30 seconds taking practice swings with the club you plan to use on the first tee. Concentrate on tempo, balance, and a full finish. Then spend the next 30 seconds relaxing and visualizing your drive.

Winterizing Your Game

After a spring, summer, and fall of steady golf, most of us go into a kind of modified winter hibernation (unless we live in a warm climate). There's a temptation to wait until spring arrives before going on a crash course to get ourselves and our strokes back into playing shape.

BODY

Our advice is to "winterize" your body and stroke. Start by timing your annual physical exam with the end of the good-weather season. That will take care of all the necessary routine checks, and it will also alert you to any conditions that would prohibit you from getting started on a winter exercise program.

Talk with a sports nutritionist or registered dietitian about a sensible weight-management program for your age group and with a trainer, coach, or physical therapist about a stretching, walking, and strengthening routine—in that order. Section 3 of this book gives specific guidelines for all three areas. Start swinging a weighted club (an old iron with a golf ball or two taped to it) as part of the program. Begin with just 10 swings a day or every other day, then build up to 20 to 25 swings during each workout. Swing from the right and left sides to equally condition both halves of your body.

The combination of stretches, walking, and low-intensity strength training puts you in better physical condition, gets you into the habit of doing something physical every day, and helps your golf game by making you stronger and more flexible. By springtime you'll be ready to go, because you've been on a full-time program for several months.

STROKES

Finally, winterize your strokes—at least your short game—by using an enclosed area like the basement to practice putting on a carpet and chipping into a small net. If not the full game, you can at least keep these two areas of your game in reasonable condition. And you'll drive your scores down more by improving the short game than by worrying about distance.

2 best-ever tips

With the possible exceptions of day traders and gamblers, golfers like to give and get tips more than anyone. Following are more than 50 suggestions from fellow golfers, teaching professionals who work with older players, and members of the PGA Senior Tour.

Trying to incorporate all this free advice at once is sure to cause more problems than it solves. But read through this section and select the information that fits your body, your strokes, your mental approach, and your ability level. You may find that the 15-handicapper in Kansas or California has something to say that's just as important as a tip from a top money winner on the tour. There's something here for everyone.

Tips from After-50 Golfers

Golfers and golf pros spend as much time watching others swing the club as they do hitting the ball themselves. As a result, just about everyone has given a tip to a friend and has gotten more than a little advice from others. We asked Golf After 50 readers to share their "best tips" with us. Here are some of them.

BEHIND THE BALL

"Good grief! There are so many tips, but one that comes to mind is: Always keep your eye/face/head just behind the ball prior to impact, no matter where it is, back or forward. Focus on the back, not the top of the ball. Good luck."

—David

READ FROM BOTH SIDES

"Always read your putt from both sides of the hole. If there are conflicting reads, trust your read from below the hole. Not only does it improve your reading of the putt, but it also forces you not to rush your putt. If it's a flat putt and you have conflicting reads, get glasses. If you have a flat putt, glasses, and conflicting reads, disregard this message."

—Steve

HANDS IN LINE

"The best golf tip I ever got was to keep my hands in line throughout the stroke whether it's a full swing, pitch, or putt. A good setup, of course, is essential. However, pushing or pulling your hands off line will almost certainly ensure that your stroke will be off target."

—Curtis

HAVE A GOOD TIME

"Surely technique and concentration are high on the list of golf instruction, but I believe in having a good time and maintaining a positive state of mind. The more fun you have, the more relaxed you are, and relaxation is the key to the swing. Being tense and aggravated can spoil your round and everybody else's. By putting fun back into golf, I believe you can relax, concentrate, and learn. It's only a game. Have a good time playing it!"

—Adonis

ONE, TWO, SWING

"My most frequent problem is that I swing too quickly. A guy passed by me on the driving range one day and gave me a tip: He told me to say, 'One, two, swing,' to myself as I started my backswing. Worked great! I now do this with every practice swing."

—James

HIT THE LITTLE BALL FIRST

"This may sound silly, but hit the little ball first. Nine out of ten times, recreational players hit the ground (the big ball—planet earth) first. So instead, hit the little ball first, then the ground. Another way to say it is, Don't hit the ground first. The only exception to this rule is when you're hitting out of a trap. Then hit the sand first, ball second."

—Don

EXHALE ON BACKSWING

"Just about the time I was turning 50, I read an article about golf and relaxation. The major point was that it's important to slowly exhale as you commence your backswing. Exhaling relaxes the big muscle groups and allows for a nice flowing swing without any change in grip tension. Now I realize that by asking someone how they breathe during their backswing, I could actually be assisting them."

—Pete

ARMS IN

"The best swing thought, I believe, is to keep your arms/hands as close to the middle of your chest as possible on the back- and forward swing (at the same time maintaining extension of your left arm). This encourages the proper turn away from the ball and increases the chance of proper timing on the downswing. Golf teachers call this 'keeping the club in front of you.' I never understood that concept. My explanation seems simpler."

—Randy

LOOK AT THE BACK OF THE HOLE

"One day, while playing in North Carolina with a guy I had never met before, I complained after the first few holes about my dilemma: I always leave my putts short. The guy casually asked if I looked at the front of the hole or the back. I said that I looked at the front. He told me that if I would look at the back of the hole, it would completely change my perspective on putting distance. It did—immediately! It is without a doubt the best tip I have had in 45 years of playing golf. Try it."

—Charlie

SMOOTH TEMPO

"My simple cure for mis-hits is to keep your swing tempo smooth—back-up-down—and keep your grip soft all the while. Back too fast and down too hard ensures a mis-hit. A tight, constricting grip just adds to the problem. I find that the 'old smoothie' swing-and-hit avoids mis-hits and promotes straight drives from the tee or the fairway."

—Adsuar

LEFT ARM TIGHT

"I'm 62 and I have to think *left arm tight to the side* on the downswing and try to finish lower. This keeps me from letting my arms separate from my body and hitting the ball on the heel of the club."

—Jack

NEW DRIVER

"I enjoy the opportunity to share my thoughts about succeeding. I just got a new driver, and feeling that I'm on the cutting edge of technology builds my confidence. I've shot my best round ever (85 in November) and look forward to playing each time I go to the course. I'm 59 and think that the next decade will be my best years of golf if I continue to be healthy and fit. It really pleased me to see an article that concurred with my choice of clubs. That only helps build my confidence that I have the best equipment."

—Elcina

LISTEN TO YOUR FEET

"Here are two tips that have always helped me play a little better golf. (1) When faced with a sidehill shot, whether it be a fairway, rough, or putt—but especially a putt—'Listen to your feet.' On the putt, your feet will tell you if you are aligned square to the hill. Then align your hips and shoulders and putt along that line. The ball will fall naturally toward the hole. With a little practice and confidence in gravity, 3-putts will turn into easy lags, with an occasional make. (2) 'Hats off in the wind.' In windy conditions (like those on the coast of Oregon), a hat can cup the wind and make the delicate art of balance even harder. Why complicate matters? Take the bloody thing off, swing easy, and enjoy."

—Robert

WORK OUT

"Work out! Upper-body strength and flexibility are essential. I'm 65 and still a 6-handicapper thanks to staying in shape and inheriting good hand–eye coordination, which has given me a sound short game."

—Roy

CONTROLLED SWING

"As I passed the 60-year mark and now have passed the 65 mark there is no question that the best tip or advice I've received is to control my swing. No matter what the equipment or what the swing might be, the ball just does not go as far as it used to when I was younger. However, by controlling the speed of my swing I find the ball does go straighter most of the time. The distance lost isn't a factor, for I'm playing out of the short grass most of the time."

—Arnie

NOT LIKE TIGER

"After 50, don't look to hit the ball like Tiger. It's not going to happen. Just be thankful you're on a golf course. What else could you ask for? Enjoy the game for all it gives you."

—Pinky

TRYING TO CLEAR A HAZARD

"I don't attempt long fairway shots that have to clear a hazard. If it takes a carry of more than 160 or 170 yards, I'll lay up and hit the short iron onto the green."

—John

THREADING THE NEEDLE

"I used to think that the best way to get out of trouble was by threading the needle through trees to get closer to the hole. Now I don't mind hitting a 90-degree angle shot back into the fairway. I'll give up a stroke and take a bogey rather than spend all day in the woods."

—Wade

CHARGING THE HOLE

"I used to charge the hole on every putt, go for the birdie, and end up 10 feet past the hole. Now if I can lag up within a couple of feet, I'll take my 2-putt and be happy."

—Jimmy

HOPING FOR THE BEST

"I try not to hit shots that I just hope will work. Instead, I concentrate on hitting shots that I actually think I'm capable of executing."

—Steve

DON'T OVERSWING

"At our age, range and motion are limited at best. Few of us can say we hold to a rigid daily routine of exercise and stretching after 50 (as much as we would like to). Overswinging will, without a doubt, put more bad shots into your game than anything else. There seems to be an urge to swing with as much force as possible. I see it in my fellow seniors day after day. Keep things as condensed as possible, firm without added stress. The more you overswing, the better your chances of doing something wrong. This game is hard enough; don't make it worse."

—A. J.

WATCH THE LABEL

"Harvey Penick said always put the label up on the ball, on the tee, and watch the label until the ball is gone. You'll be surprised how much more accurate you will be if you practice this method. This teaches you to keep your head down."

—Walter

Tips from Teaching Professionals

Following, in no particular order, are selected teaching gems provided by our guest pros and other teaching professionals experienced in working with after-50 players. We've said it before: Just choose those best suited for your game. The ones you can't use may work for someone else.

HUNKER IN THE BUNKER

"Hunker in the bunker. A good setup for bunker play means getting down low in the bunker with your buttocks, your knees flexed a bit more than normal. There should be a fairly abrupt wrist hinge on the backswing, then a big backswing, contact 2 to 3 inches behind the ball, and a big follow-through."

> — Eric Eshelman, director of instruction
> Robert Trent Jones Golf Trail
> Birmingham, Alabama

GRIPPING THE CLUB

"Make sure that when you take your grip, the club is in the fingers of your hands, not the palm, and that you can see two knuckles of your left hand with the thumb at the right center of the shaft.

Having this grip will give you more flexibility in the wrist, add leverage to your swing, and allow you to square the club with less effort. For those of you who have felt your swing getting shorter and the ball flight lower, we suggest a 10-finger (baseball) grip instead of an overlapping grip."

—Bill Moretti, director of instruction
The Academy of Golf Dynamics
Austin, Texas

THINK 2 SHOTS AHEAD

"The next time you're faced with the following situations, think 2 shots ahead:

✓ Sometimes it's better to lay up on an approach shot that leaves you a full shot to the green (if possible), instead of hoping you'll carry trouble.

✓ The next time you're in a deep bunker with a big lip, go for the shallow end and just get the ball onto the green.

✓ Aim for the middle of the green instead of a pin tucked in the corner surrounded by big bunkers.

✓ Take one more club for all approach shots. After-50 golfers love to inch their way up to the green. Challenge yourself. Be long on your approach shots.

✓ For fairway bunkers, your target may not necessarily be the green. It might be the fairway. Select a club that will get the ball out of the sand and put you in a good position for your next shot.

✓ The next time you go to the driving range, practice your trouble shots. Try to think what will happen the next time you're on the golf course."

—Judy Alvarez, manager
PGA Learning Center Programs
Port St. Lucie, Florida

WHEN TO FOCUS

"Don't try to stay totally focused during an entire round of golf. It takes only a few seconds to hit a shot, and that's the time you need to pull yourself back into focus. Find a way to trigger your concentration when you need it the most. For Palmer, it was hitching his pants. For someone else, it might be tugging on a glove or a cap.

Whatever your trigger is, it should be a signal to yourself that it's time to fully concentrate on the next shot."

> —Fred Griffin, director
> Grand Cypress Academy of Golf
> Orlando, Florida

LEVEL SHOULDERS EQUALS DRIVING DISTANCE

"Senior golfers who begin to lose distance try to get it back by swinging more with their hands and arms. I tell them to start the swing by keeping their shoulders level, but it's not a very common concept because, on TV, the left shoulder always appears to be lower than the right one. That's simply because the shoulders are being rotated around the spine, which is a tilted axis. If you keep your shoulders level during the turn, that gets the weight more on the right foot at the top of the swing. Once you finish your turn, you can finish your backswing by cocking your wrists and letting your right arm fold. I understand that older golfers can't turn as much as they once could, but if they turn as much as they can, they'll see that they can swing much easier and hit the ball farther."

> —Bill Welson, teaching professional
> Hyatt Bear Creek Golf Club
> Dallas, Texas

RIGHT FOOT BACK

"In order to make the turn a bit easier and to deliver the club from the inside (rather than outside to inside), combine turning your left foot out with flaring your right foot and pulling it back from the original stance line. In other words, the right foot will be slightly behind the straight line that would normally be formed between the toes of both feet. From that setup position, you ought to be able to hit a good draw."

> —Tom Losinger, director of instruction
> Bridge Mill Athletic Club, Canton, Georgia

PUTTING AND CHIPPING

"For two weeks, devote 90 percent of your practice time to chipping and putting, and only 10 percent to the full swing. If you do this, your 95 will turn into a 90. I guarantee it."

> —Harvey Penick
> from *Harvey Penick's Little Red Book*

STAY IN YOUR POSTURE

"The number one piece of advice for after-50 golfers is to exercise. Stretch the body out as much as you can. The second tip is to stay in your posture as you swing the club. That means don't straighten up, raise your head, or otherwise abandon your good-swing technique. Senior golfers lose their flexibility, and many start to come out of their posture because they don't have the flexibility to stay in it."

> —Bruce Schalk, head pro
> Marine Park Golf Course
> Brooklyn, New York

GEAR DOWN

"On the practice tee, start with your present full-speed swing and proceed to gear down by 10 percent after every 5 shots. Notice what happens when you're at around 70 to 90 percent of effort. At this point, you'll fully appreciate the concept of conservation of energy. The ball will travel close to, if not the same distance as, your 100 percent swing, but with greater accuracy and less effort."

> —Dr. Evan Brody, sports psychophysiologist
> Olney, Maryland

LOSS OF BALANCE

"I don't see that much difference in golfers when they turn 50, but after 70 some golfers experience a fear of falling. As a result, they play more flat-footed. I simply ask them if they're afraid of falling, or I have them go through a few swings with a regular finish. If I see them lose their balance, I just put a stop to it and suggest a shorter swing. I also advise them to use something at home with which they can practice their swing to a full finish near a chair or sofa. Then, if they lose their balance, they can grab the chair. If balance continues to be a problem, they just have to accept it, shorten their swings, and settle for less distance."

> —George Kelnhofer, head professional
> Atlanta Golf Center
> Norcross, Georgia

LESS PRESSURE, MORE SPEED

"More distance off the tee is the result of properly applied club-head speed into the back of the golf ball. To increase club-head speed, most golfers need to decrease their grip pressure and forearm tension. Light grip pressure (about a 5 on a scale of 1 to 10) allows the golfer to freely swing the club back and through in combination with body timing. Excessive tension in the body severely restricts this motion."

> —Craig Bunker, vice president
> Jacobs' Golf Schools
> Scottsdale, Arizona

AVOID WRISTINESS

"The sense of touch on putts may not be as good in senior players as it was when they were younger. To compensate for this, you shouldn't be afraid to try long putters or a cross-handed putting style to keep the wristiness out of your stroke. Anything that will give you more confidence on those 3-, 4-, and 5-foot putts is an advantage. Also, instead of banging drive after drive after drive on the practice tee, spend some of that time putting, where you can really save strokes."

> —Chris McSpadden, head pro
> TPC at Sugarloaf
> Duluth, Georgia

GET A PGA PRO

"The best golf tip is to find a PGA teaching professional and develop a long-term program."

> —Rick Martino, director of instruction
> PGA of America

Tips from Senior Tour Players, Former Players, and Legends

You've read tips from other after-50 golfers and from teaching professionals. Now you're going to get some inexpensive advice from former players, voices from the past, and members of the Senior PGA Tour. The last group plays with golfers like us every week in pro-am tournaments, watching us whack the ball around; their observations about our games might help us shave a stroke or two per round. Some of these tips were given directly to us during telephone, fax, or e-mail interviews. In other cases, we found tips previously published and summarized them for this section of the book.

STRETCH, STRETCH, STRETCH

"Stretch, stretch, and then stretch while using light weights for maintaining strength. Eat sensibly and try to promote good general health. Maintain a positive attitude about your mind and body."

—Hale Irwin

"The major difference between young and older golfers is loss of flexibility. Specific stretching exercises that are designed to improve the range of motion used in the golf swing would be very beneficial to the senior player."

—Larry Nelson

"Get on an exercise program now if you aren't on one. The muscles become less flexible, and it becomes more difficult to make a full turn as we get older. Any strengthening and stretching exercise will delay the inevitable loss of strength and flexibility."

—Tom Kite

ESTABLISH A WORKOUT ROUTINE

"I established a workout routine with a personal trainer and have stayed with the program over the years. It really paid off once I joined the Senior Tour, which is a very demanding season of golf. Keeping myself physically strong is more important than anything I've ever done."

—Vicente Hernandez

PREPARING FOR A TOURNAMENT

"I see lots of amateurs who play way too much golf before a tournament starts. They're used to playing perhaps three or four days a week, but start playing almost every day to prepare for competition. By the time the tournament starts, they've worn themselves out. It's better to stay in the same routine that you're used to than to get run down physically and mentally just because you've entered a club tournament or a pro-am event."

—Butch Baird

WARMING UP

"When warming up before a round, make the last shot you hit on the practice tee the same as the first shot you have to hit on the course."

—Ken Venturi, from *Ken Venturi's Stroke Savers*

TRANSFERRING WEIGHT

"There is one thing I noticed about every great player. They all transferred their weight well. When the club went back to the right, their weight was on the right side. When the club went through to the follow-through, the weight was on the left side. I've never seen a great golfer leave his weight on the right side. A lot of weekend golfers leave all of their weight back as they hit the ball and then move to their right side for the finishing position."

—Gary Player, adapted from CBS
Sportsline/PGATour.com/Golf Web

INTERMEDIATE TARGET

"First, pick an intermediate target for every shot. Instead of focusing on a pin 150 yards away, pick a spot—a divot, hole, or discoloration—about 10 yards in front of your ball along the target line. Square your club face to the intermediate target. It's easier to be precise when the target is close. If you are square to the intermediate target you are square to your ultimate target as well."

—Nancy Lopez, from *Golf Magazine*

LOWER-BODY MOVEMENT

"One of the most important things in a golf swing to me is the movement of the lower body from the top of the swing. You start with your knees and hips. From the top of the swing, you move the lower part of your body first—not your shoulders, but your lower body. Let your arms and hands follow the lower body, which will bring you into the hitting position. But the first move from the top of the swing is made with the knees. Then release your upper body at the bottom in the hitting area."

—Ben Hogan, adapted from CBS
Sportsline/PGATour.com/Golf Web

TOO MUCH LOFT AROUND THE GREEN

"Senior players want to use too much loft when the ball is close to the green. They try to hit underneath the ball to get it into the air. I believe you should take the least amount of loft that can get you over the fringe around a green and let it run as a putt. Play the ball back in your stance and never let the club come underneath the ball. The only time you should do that is when you're pitching. For anything close to the green, use less loft. Farther away from the green, use more loft."

—Billy Casper

SHANKING

"The most common cause of shanking, particularly on short shots, is making a backswing that is too flat. To correct this, practice trying to keep the club vertical on the backswing and allow the club head simply to drop on the ball."

—Sam Snead, from *Golf Digest*

80 TO 90 PERCENT EFFORT

"While I swing close to full on most drives, I use 85 to 90 percent effort for the middle irons and about 80 percent on the short irons. I stay within myself and concentrate on making clean contact, which makes the ball fly a predictable distance. So ignore what others may be hitting and play your approach shots with plenty of club and a smooth, controlled swing. I promise you'll get the ball closer and score lower."

—Gil Morgan, senior golfer, www.golfonline

WHEN PRACTICING

"When practicing, use the club that gives you the most trouble, and do not waste your time in knocking a ball about with the tool that gives you the most satisfaction and with which you rarely make a bad stroke."

—Harry Vardon, from *The Complete Golfer*

FAIRWAY BUNKERS

"This is a situation where you're 50 to 55 yards out in a fairway bunker. You're on a par-5 hole, and the bunkers are guarding against the layup shot. If necessary, lay back another 30 yards and leave yourself 80 yards into the green. Don't try to force a shot into a narrow gap. However, if you find yourself in this position, here's how to get out. Don't take any sand before the ball. Play it like a pitch shot from the fairway. If you hit 1/2 inch too much sand, you'll come up short of the green. So it's very important to catch the ball first with your club. To do that, start by putting the ball back in your stance. The second thing is to keep your weight forward. Don't try to help the ball get in the air by putting your weight back and getting under it. This weight-forward stance will help you catch the ball on the downswing."

—Jay Haas, adapted from CBS Sportsline/PGATour.com/Golf Web

FROM A BUNKER

"From a good lie in the sand, you must open the sand wedge. When the ball is buried, you must square the blade. I see more bad shots from seniors because they violate these rules than for any other reason."

—Gary Player, from *Golf Begins at 50*

PUTTING SPEED

"You have to hit each putt so that the ball rolls at the right speed. If you don't have the speed, you don't know where to aim. Two feet or 40 feet, your aim must be to hit the ball at a pace that will see it finish 14 to 18 inches beyond the hole."

—Gary McCord, from *Golf for Dummies*

PUTTING FOCUS

"When you rotate your eyes to the ball just before beginning your stroke, stay focused on the back of the ball. I wouldn't call it staring. I just feel I'm focused on the back of the ball. That helps you see the whole picture—the ball and the path of the putt."

—Jim Colbert, from *Senior Golfer*

SAVE 1

"*Save 1.* That means I try to think about saving 1 stroke per round that I wouldn't normally save. It might be chipping, putting, or any stroke that will turn things around for me. The Save 1 goal puts me on alert not to take any shot lightly."

—Butch Baird

3 older and stronger

"The most important thing I have done since joining the Senior Tour," says Argentina's Vicente Hernandez, "is establish a work-out routine to keep myself physically strong." We should all follow Vicente's example. Getting older doesn't have to mean getting weaker. In this section there are practical suggestions regarding the things we can do to maintain or increase strength, power, flexibility, endurance, and perhaps how far we hit our drives. From do-them-at-home resistance exercises to stretching routines, advice about a walking program, and hints on shopping for exercise equipment, there's something here that will help you slow the aging process and add speed and power to your swing.

Never Too Old

You are not too old to start lifting weights. Don't skip this section! We know what you're thinking, because we thought the same thing. Mention "lifting weights" and we start getting mental pictures of health clubs, barbells, machines, and television infomercial gadgets. Wrong.

If you can afford a couple of small dumbbells or elastic cords, and if you can find half an hour in your schedule every other day, you can start an in-house exercise program that will change your life and your golf game. Not convinced? Wayne Wescott and Tom Baechle, authors of *Strength Training Past 50,* give us lots of reasons why we should strength train. Surprisingly, only three of them have anything to do with strength.

KEEP WHAT YOU HAVE

"Unless we exercise, we lose 5 pounds of muscle tissue every decade of adult life," explain the authors. "Because muscles are the engines of the body, it's like dropping from an eight-cylinder car to a six to a four to a motor scooter."

METABOLIZE

If you lose muscle tissue, your metabolic rate (the process that burns calories) decreases at the same time. A strength-training program increases your metabolic rate and produces a higher level of calorie use.

ADD MUSCLE TISSUE

You can add muscle tissue at any age. According to a study at Ohio University, men over 60 can become 80 percent stronger if they start doing high-intensity weight training. Seniors can gain strength at the same rate as men in their 20s. Sixty days of strength training, 30 minutes a day, two or three days a week sees an average gain of nearly 4 pounds of muscle in men and almost 2 pounds in women.

CUT THE FAT

A strength-training program is a triple play. A modest home exercise program adds muscle, reduces fat, and helps you lose weight, even if you don't reduce your calorie intake.

STRONG BONES

Several studies have shown that strength training maintains bone strength, increases bone density, and lessens the probability of osteoporosis.

THE DIABETES CONNECTION

The body's ability to use glucose is closely related to the risk of diabetes. Exercise in general, and strength training in particular, appear to benefit this process. Bottom line: Strength training may indirectly decrease the likelihood of developing adult-onset diabetes.

REDUCE COLON CANCER RISK

The longer food stays in the gastrointestinal system, the greater the risk of colon cancer. Strength training can speed up the transit process by 56 percent. Enough said.

LOWER BLOOD PRESSURE

Contrary to what you may have read, sensible strength training does not raise resting blood pressure. Instead, a combination of moderate exercises and proper breathing can produce a long-term blood pressure decrease.

YOUR ACHING BACK

If you haven't experienced low-back pain yet, get ready. There is an 80 percent chance that you will, and the figure is even higher among golfers. A study at the University of Florida showed that 80 percent of low-back-pain patients had less pain after a few weeks of strength training.

YOUR ACHING JOINTS

If your back doesn't get you, your joints probably will. Most of us will develop some degree of osteoarthritis, which has a direct effect on how we move and swing a club on the golf course. Stronger muscles can help improve joint health and reduce pain.

That's it—our sermon to convince you to start a strength training program, whatever your age. Now you can't hide behind your age as an excuse for playing poorly. Do something about it. Not for us, but for yourself.

Strength Training 101

Those of you who bought into the need for a strength-training program need specific instructions to get started. Here they are.

Invest about $40 in a basic dumbbell (not barbell) set. A dumbbell is generally lighter than a barbell and has a short bar that's just wide enough for your hand to comfortably fit between the weighted ends. (A barbell is longer and holds a group of weights on each end.) If you shop around, you may find used dumbbells that cost less than $40. That should get you two bars with locks and four 10-pound, four 5-pound, four 2 1/2-pound, and four 1 1/4-pound plates.

Here are frequently asked questions about strength training, followed by some short answers.

How much weight should I lift?
Enough weight so that you can lift it 8 to 12 times.

How many sets of the 8 to 12 repetitions should I complete?
During the first week or two, start with one set for each type of lift. Later, move up to two or three sets.

How many days a week should I lift?
Two or three nonconsecutive days. Give your muscles time to recover.

As I get stronger, how much weight should I add?
No more than 2 1/2 pounds on each bar. Lift the new amount for
a couple of weeks before adding to the load again.

Ready for the first lift? It's called the Dumbbell Chest Fly, and it'll
make you stronger in the chest and shoulder area.

CHEST FLY

- ✓ Lie back on a narrow weight bench (or floor, table,
  ottoman, or very firm mattress) with your knees bent
  at 90 degrees.

- ✓ Keep your head, shoulders, and hips in contact with the
  bench, and your feet in contact with the floor.

- ✓ Hold the dumbbells out to your sides, elbows bent, so that
  your palms face each other.

- ✓ Exhale and push the weights upward at the same time to a
  position over your chest with your elbows slightly flexed.

- ✓ Now lower the weights gradually until your upper arms are
  parallel to the floor.

LATERAL RAISE

- ✓ Standing with your feet spread at hip width, hold the
  dumbbells with your palms down and facing the outside
  of your legs, elbows slightly bent.

- ✓ Exhale and lift both weights slowly until your arms
  are parallel to the floor.

✓ Inhale as you lower the dumbbells just as slowly until you return to the starting position.

That's it. Work on these two upper-body lifts for a couple of weeks. Don't get antsy and try to do too much. You may be a little sore at first, but you'll start noticing a strength gain within two or three weeks. Stay with the program and gradually add to it.

When you're ready to expand your training, here's one more lift for your arms and two for your lower body, which is just as important to your golf swing as upper-body strength. Remember the following guidelines:

✓ Enough weight to lift 8 to 12 times without pain.

✓ One set of 8 to 12 repetitions the first week, then increase to two or three sets.

✓ Three times a week with a day of rest in between.

✓ Increase the load by no more than 2 1/2 pounds every two weeks.

DUMBBELL CURL

✓ Hold the weights with your arms straight and your palms facing your legs; your feet should be spread to the width of your hips.

✓ Exhale and bring the dumbbells upward at the same time toward your shoulders. Rotate your wrists so your palms face your chest.

✓ Inhale and lower the weights to the starting position.

HEEL RAISE

✓ Hold the dumbbells at your sides with your palms facing in.

✓ Stand on a stable surface approximately 4 inches high—stair steps, for example.

✓ With your head up, shoulders back, back straight, and weight on the balls of your feet, go up on your toes as you exhale.

✓ Then lower your heels as far as you comfortably can while inhaling.

DUMBBELL SQUAT

✓ Hold the dumbbells at your sides with your palms inward.

✓ With your head up and your shoulders and back straight, slowly bend your knees until your thighs are parallel to the floor.

✓ If balance is a problem, position your back and hips against a wall for support.

✓ Exhale as you slowly return to the standing-straight-up position.

✓ Be especially careful on this one not to lift too much or move too fast.

Now you have our two-part starter kit for a golf-after-50 strength-training program. Give it time to work and gradually increase the load.

Sticking with the Program

Okay, you bought into the golf-after 50 weight-training ideas just outlined. You understand that at our age, we have two choices: We can get older and weaker, or we can get older and stronger. You decided on the second option.

SET GOALS

Now the problem is sticking with it. Fifty percent of the people who begin an exercise program drop out within six months. How can we remain in the half that continues? "Set goals," advises Penn State sports psychologist David Yukelson. "Beginning exercisers often try to do too much too quickly. Others set goals that are not consistent with their age or with the amount of time they have to give to a program. Serious exercisers are committed, but they establish goals that are realistic."

RECOGNIZE THE OBSTACLES

Recognize the obstacles. Whether they're real or imagined, we have to deal with them. For most of us, time, travel, expense, availability of facilities, and work demands are great excuses for not spending a few minutes taking care of ourselves. But once we identify the barriers, we can develop plans to overcome them. You've done it in your work all your life. Why not take the same approach with your health?

BOOK IT

Make your strength-training program a part of your schedule. If you wait for free time, you won't have any. Block out 15 to 30 minutes two or three times a week. If you can't do that, you're working too hard, anyway. Slow down and get stronger.

If your job requires travel, look for hotel, public, or club facilities in cities away from home. If the cost of joining a health club is unreasonable, look into lower-cost memberships at YMCA, YWCA, college, or church facilities. Better yet, spend a few dollars for a set of dumbbells and use them in your own golf-after-50 home gym. Monthly dues are waived and better spent on green fees.

ENJOY IT

Says Yukelson, "People are not likely to continue an activity if they don't enjoy it." Not everyone enjoys lifting weights. Alternate your weight-training program with something you enjoy doing, something that meets your needs, and something that fits your lifestyle. Weight training plus golf may be enough. But weight training two or three days a week, playing golf two or three days a week, and doing one other physical activity (like walking or swimming) would put you in an elite group.

Understanding the benefits of starting a strength program was a great first step. Actually starting a program was the second. Now go for the big one and make it last. If you get past the first six months, your new exercise program will probably become part of the rest of your life. And that life is likely to be a longer, healthier one.

Lifting Without Weights

After-50 golfers need to maintain strength and flexibility as much as or more than younger players. But lifting free weights or working out on machines requires equipment, time, money, and space that most seniors are not willing to commit. Here's an option.

ELASTIC BANDS

"Some people are simply reluctant to lift weights," says Dr. Thomas Baechle, co-author of *Strength Training Past 50,* "but they don't seem to mind working out with elastic bands. The advantages of rubber cords include low cost, safety, versatility, and the little amount of space that they occupy when traveling."

Pharmacies and medical supply stores sell oversized rubber bands for about $2 a foot. Theraband is a common brand name. It comes in colors that correspond to light, medium, and heavy resistance and is sold in lengths of 6 feet or more. A band can be cut to any length. Handles are sold to attach to each end, but most people just wrap the ends around their hands.

Here are three upper-body exercises that are useful for the arms, shoulders, and back. With each exercise, begin with three sets of five repetitions and increase the number of reps by one each week.

BICEPS CURL

Place the cord on the floor or ground and stand with your feet comfortably separated on the middle of the cord. Reach down, grasp the ends of the cord, and wrap them around your hands. Now stand straight up, flex your arms at the elbow joints so that there's no slack in the cord, and bring your hands up (palms up) and toward your shoulders before slowly returning to the starting position.

LAT PULLDOWN

Tie a knot at the center of the cord and loop the knotted portion over the top of a door. Close the door so that the knot is firmly in place on the outside and the two cord ends are hanging down on your side. Grasp the ends of the cords and hold them out to your sides so that your upper and lower arms form a right angle. Now pull down on the cords as if you're trying to put your elbows in your back pockets. Return to the starting position.

SEATED ROW

Wrap the middle of the cord around a post or some other fixture that won't move. From a seated position, grasp the ends of the cords with your hands in a position so that your elbows are even with your body. Pull on the cords, moving your elbows back behind your body. Again, do three sets of five reps, then gradually increase the number of repetitions.

Senior Stretches

Your teaching professional knows better than anyone. Golfers over 50 lose flexibility, and the loss not only causes injuries but also limits the distance we can hit the ball—and that affects what we shoot. Most of us would rather deal with pain than a bad round.

But you don't have to do either. There are ways to maintain the range of motion you now have and to slow down the natural loss of flexibility. The following simple stretches can be done before you leave home or after you arrive at a club or course.

These stretches require no equipment and little time, and they can realistically be performed by golfers of any age—even ours. To work, they must be done on a daily basis. Hold each stretch for 10 seconds and repeat it two more times, or hold the stretch for one 30-second period.

KNEES TO CHEST
(FOR THE LOWER BACK AND TRUNK)

Here's one you can do while lying in bed, flat on your back. It's our kind of exercise, and it's great for the lower back. Slowly bring your knees toward your chest. When they get within reach, grasp your legs over or under the knees and pull them closer. Don't try to go too far. Just work on improving slightly from week to week.

KNEE FLEX
(FOR THE LEGS AND LOWER BODY)

Hold on to a wall, rail, or post for balance with your right hand. Lean forward and slightly bend your left leg while flexing the right knee so that your lower leg comes up behind and toward your buttocks. Now grab your right ankle (or at least the end of your trousers) with your left hand. Pull your heel upward and slightly across, hold, then repeat the exercise using the opposite arms and legs.

DOWNSHIFT YOUR HIPS
(FOR THE LEGS AND TRUNK)

Stand with your hands on your hips or knees. Keep your heels on the floor, feet parallel to each other. Take a deep breath, let the air out, and flex your knees so that your hips sink downward. When you feel that your weight has shifted, hold the position, then slowly return to the starting position.

DOOR STRETCH
(FOR THE SHOULDERS AND UPPER BODY)

Stand facing a corner of the room or an open doorway with your feet staggered. Lift your arms up to each side of the corner or door to a point where your elbows are slightly lower than your shoulders. Now lean your whole body forward, keeping your feet flat on the floor.

FORWARD LEAN
(FOR TRUNK AND SHOULDERS)

Sit on a chair, legs together, feet flat on the floor, hands on hips, and thumbs facing forward. Bend forward at the waist until the upper part of your body is resting on (or close to) your knees. Now move your elbows forward and toward each other until you feel tension. That's far enough. Slowly return to the sitting-up position. Try to increase the length of the stretch each day.

OVERHEAD SIDE STRETCH (FOR THE TRUNK,
UPPER BODY, SHOULDERS, AND ARMS)

Start with your feet about shoulder width apart, hands clasped together and held above your head. Lean to one side at the waist and lower your outstretched arms as far as you can (without feeling pain or tightness) to that side. Hold for 30 seconds, then do the same thing on the other side.

Okay. Now you have a six-pack for the road. Do these stretches (or some of them) every morning before you play and every night before you go to bed. All six combined take only three minutes and there's some overlap, so you could get by with three, four, or five stretches. We're not offering a money-back guarantee, but we know they've worked for others; they might help you to stay loose enough to swing easy and pain-free.

The Case
for Walking

It may be inconvenient, it may slow down play a bit, and it may even be against the rules at some clubs, but the arguments for walking instead of riding in carts are stronger than ever.

A study of 55 golfers aged 48 to 64 years old reported in the *American Journal of Medicine* found that those who walked 18 holes two or three times a week for five months instead of riding increased their aerobic endurance, lost an average of 3 pounds more than a control group, and had lower body fat along with higher levels of HDL—the good kind of cholesterol.

MODEST BENEFITS

Dr. Jari Parkkari, one of the Finnish researchers who conducted the study, said that golf is a low- to moderate-intensity exercise that qualifies as a health-enhancing activity. He added that walking in any form, golf or otherwise, as a pattern of behavior provides a reasonable and safe way to gain modest health benefits. Parkkari noted that the results studied were short term and not a predictor of long-term risk of disease. Still, walking the golf course may prevent general weakness and reduce the likelihood of falls and fractures.

The problem with walking is that most people don't walk often enough or fast enough to achieve significant benefits. The Centers for Disease Control and Prevention has data that indicate only 25 percent of those who do walk reach the "brisk" category.

If walking on the course, in the neighborhood, or at the mall is your primary form of exercise, don't worry about distance. If you walk fast enough, long enough, and often enough, the distance factor will take care of itself. How fast? There are too many variables for us to list a number for every after-50 golfer, but 3 1/2 miles per hour is the most commonly recommended pace. How long? Thirty minutes. How often? At least three times a week; preferably four.

MORE THAN MODEST BENEFITS

If you want to get past "modest health benefits," gradually work up to a speed that gets your heart rate somewhere between 65 and 85 percent of maximum. To determine your target heart rate, subtract your age from 220, then multiply that figure by 0.65, then 0.85. Every heart rate between the two numbers qualifies as aerobic exercise if you meet the time and frequency criteria.

There are degrees of benefits from walking. You get what you put into it. Walking is better than nothing. Even walking at a leisurely pace provides the emotional advantage of seeing the world in a calming way. Walking during a round of golf is better than riding a cart. Walking at a brisk pace several times a week, on or off the golf course, is better than walking, stopping, and swinging a club.

Buying Home Exercise Equipment

For most after-50 golfers, playing the game is all the exercise they get. Some of those who ride carts while playing are conscientious enough to engage in a walking program in addition to time spent on the course. And then there are those who go the extra mile by using home exercise equipment.

For those of you who are thinking about purchasing equipment to use at home, here are some suggestions that may save you money and benefit your fitness program.

MEDICAL ADVICE

If you, like most of us, have an existing condition that could be affected by exercise, get some medical advice before you buy or work out on any machine. "Golfers who have low-back pain, arthritis, or even a total joint replacement can still exercise on a regular basis," says Dr. Nicholas DiNubile of the University of Pennsylvania. "But they should consult a sports medicine physician about the type of equipment best suited to their needs."

GOALS

Match your equipment to your fitness goals. Educate yourself about the benefits of each type of equipment in terms of what it will do for your heart, your muscles, or the other systems of your body.

AVOID IMPULSE BUYING

Don't buy exercise equipment on impulse. You've waited this long: a little more time won't hurt you. Compare features and shop for value. In some cases, equipment that's sold under different names and at different prices is made by the same company. Don't rule out secondhand exercise equipment stores. Most people stop using machines after six months and get rid of them at deep discounts.

TESTING, TESTING

Test the machine before you buy it, and wear your workout clothes during the test. DiNubile advises us to go through a workout at the store that simulates the intensity of a home workout. But be careful: Don't do too much, too soon.

THE COMFORT FACTOR

Pay attention to how you feel using the equipment. Some combinations of machines, bodies, and movements just don't mix. Don't force your body into positions and routines for which it is not suited.

COST VS QUALITY

Don't equate money spent with the quality of a workout. Says DiNubile, "One of the best home workouts for building strength can be performed using rubber tubes or bands."

EVALUATE ADS

Take a critical look at equipment advertisements. There is no single piece of equipment that offers a total workout, regardless of what the infomercial says.

4 to your health

Growing older, as someone said, isn't for sissies. This section discusses some of the common medical concerns of senior golfers, such as dehydration, managing our weight, taking care of our hearts, and playing when we don't feel well. There are also suggestions for protecting ourselves from the sun, from lightning, and from the high-pressure sales pitches that promise to make all of our aches and pains go away—for the right price.

Don't Trust Your Thirst

When it comes to beverages, golfers, especially those over 50, have two problems. The first is that we don't drink enough fluids, and the second is that many of the fluids we do take in don't do us any good.

A study by the Brita Company revealed that as many as three out of four Americans drink less fluid than they should. When athletes don't replace the fluids they lose naturally, performance suffers. Most of us wait for thirst to tell us to drink something—and by then it's too late. We can lose 1 percent of body weight before thirst kicks in. A 3 percent weight loss caused by poor hydration can dramatically affect our performance on a golf course. After 50, thirst becomes an even less reliable indicator of good hydration.

NEGATIVE HYDRATION

We can't count coffee, tea, soft drinks, and alcohol in the eight glasses of fluids we're supposed to consume on a daily basis. If a beverage contains caffeine or alcohol (both diuretics), we get a net fluid intake of just three glasses instead of eight. The other five are excreted in urine. It's called negative hydration.

Try to drink a quart of caffeine-free, alcohol-free fluid for every 1,000 calories you expend every day. Assuming that you're on schedule with fluids on the day you play golf, drink 4 to 8 ounces

5 to 10 minutes before you start a round or do any kind of physical activity. (A gulp is approximately equal to an ounce.) While you're playing, drink 4 to 8 ounces every 15 or 20 minutes. After a round, drink 16 ounces for every pound of weight lost. Finally, within 24 hours of exercise on a hot day, make sure you've replaced all the weight you lost the day before.

Food and Performance

Some golfers don't get it. They keep eating the way they did when they were younger, then wonder why they're having problems during or after a round of golf. Eating the wrong food, eating too much food, or eating at the wrong time can have a negative effect on the way you play golf. The older you get, the stronger the connection between food and performance becomes.

The following chart connects common health and exercise problems with possible causes. Remember that people react to foods and beverages in different ways.

PROBLEM	FOOD THAT MAY CAUSE THE PROBLEM
fatigue	not enough calories
	not enough carbohydrates
	not enough iron or fluids
dehydration	not enough fluids
	alcoholic beverages
	caffeine
heat cramps	not enough sodium or potassium
	not enough magnesium or chloride
stomach cramps	excessive antacids
	NSAIDs

nervousness	caffeine
	herbal stimulants
headache	MSG (monosodium glutamate)
	red wine
	chocolate
sluggishness	too much sugar
	high-fat diet

Losing Weight

If someone offered you a formula for permanently cutting 4 strokes off your handicap, would you accept it? Okay, if someone offered you a formula for permanently losing weight, would you accept it? What if you had to choose between the two? Never mind. We don't want to know. Let's stick with the weight-loss formula.

When we think of losing weight, the thought of cutting calorie intake by 3,500 just to lose 1 pound can be intimidating. Planning weight loss on a daily basis with a combined program of moderate calorie reduction and increased exercise is easier to handle.

Reducing your intake of calories by 250 a day while at the same time expending 250 additional calories produces a net difference of 500. At that rate, 1 pound of permanent weight loss a week and 4 pounds a month seems manageable.

HERE'S THE PLAN

Below are diet and exercise options suggested by the Mayo Clinic to manage weight on a daily basis. The most practical one for golfers is to burn up 250 to 300 extra calories a day by walking at least part of the course. If you share a cart with someone, consider walking every other hole or walking to get to the next shot at least some of the time.

Sixty total minutes of walking, even chopped up into small segments, can make a difference. Here are some other ways to eat less and exercise more to lose those 4 pounds. Maybe losing the weight will help us cut some strokes, also.

FOODS WITH APPROXIMATELY 250–300 CALORIES

1 candy bar or 1 bowl ice cream

2 cookies or 2 tsp. butter or margarine

2 12-oz. bottles beer

2 12-oz. sweetened soft drinks

3–4 oz. meat

EXERCISE EXPENDING APPROXIMATELY 250–300 CALORIES

60 min. walking (total)

50 min. gardening

30 min. lap swimming

25 min. jogging

25 min. cycling

Friendly Fat

Fat has gotten a bad rap. Sports nutritionists are now reminding after-50 golfers and other athletes that fat is an essential part of our diets. In addition to being the most concentrated source of energy, fat cushions our organs, insulates us against cold weather, and moves at least four vitamins to places where they can be used by the body.

In the right amounts, fat is an important part of preparing for any kind of sports participation. But "in the right amounts" is the problem.

30 PERCENT OR LESS

Most of us get 40 percent of our calories from fat. That's too much. We should be getting 20 to 30 percent of our calories from fat. How can we keep track of how many calories we're consuming in fat? The easiest way is to limit the majority of foods that we buy and eat to those that have 30 percent or less of their calories in the form of fat. Just read the labels. To play it safe, look for products that contain less than 25 percent of calories as fat.

EVEN SPLIT

The second way to make sure fat is golf-after-50-friendly is to split 30 percent evenly among saturated, polyunsaturated, and mono-unsaturated fats. That gets a little complicated, but it's still manageable. Saturated fats are the least healthy. Limit them by cutting down on cookies, cakes, solid vegetable oils, some margarines, and any foods that contain hydrogenated vegetable oils.

Polyunsaturated fat is heart-healthier than saturated fat. Get it in vegetable oils such as safflower oil, sunflower oil, corn oil, soybean oil, and cottonseed oil. Some margarines are made with polyunsaturated fat. Look for them the next time you shop for groceries.

The healthiest fat of all is monounsaturated. It's found in olive oil, canola oil, peanut oil, salmon, mackerel, halibut, swordfish, black cod, rainbow trout, and shellfish. This type of fat is good because it helps lower LDL cholesterol—the bad kind—while it stabilizes the level of good cholesterol, HDL.

Here's a summary of ways to keep your relationship with fat friendly and healthy:

✓ Choose foods that have 30 percent or less of their calories in fat.

✓ Maintain a balance among the three types of fat.

✓ Buy soft tub margarines, not the kinds that come in stick form.

✓ Limit your use of liquid vegetable oils.

✓ Eat small portions (4 to 6 ounces) of lean beef.

✓ Cut back on any foods that contain hydrogenated vegetable oils.

✓ Get most of your calories from carbohydrates, not fat.

Weight Creep

"Golfers talk about course management, but rarely about diet management," says Dr. Chris Rosenbloom, a spokesperson for the American Dietetic Association and professor of nutrition at Georgia State University. "Energy (calorie) needs decline with age. If you continue to take in the same amount of calories that you did when you were younger, you're probably going to put on weight. I call it 'weight creep,' and it sets the stage for heart disease, high blood pressure, and diabetes."

Rosenbloom gives us three simple strategies to avoid weight creep. The first is to always eat breakfast, even if you have an early tee time. She suggests bagels, cereal with skim milk, fruit, and fruit juices for energy. If you skip breakfast, you're headed for a nutritional meltdown by the ninth hole and an overeating binge at the end of the round.

Her second tip is to drink 2 cups of water or juice before tee time and a gulp (ounce) every 10 to 15 minutes—even in cold weather. Sports drinks are good for replacing water, nutrients, and electrolytes. Avoid drinks with caffeine, because they can contribute to dehydration.

If you're really serious about fluids and performance, take a closer look at your alcohol consumption. It's a high-calorie depressant that affects reasoning, reaction time, coordination, vision, alertness, and hydration—or rather, dehydration. Drinking any amount before or during a round can have an adverse effect on your performance. Moderate consumption after a round shouldn't cause any health problems, but quench your thirst first with water, not beer.

Back to Rosenbloom. "Don't wipe out all the benefits you gained from exercising on the golf course by eating high-fat snack foods from a vending machine, in the pro shop, or at the clubhouse grill. Fruits, bagels, and pretzels are great snack foods. If you need a light meal instead of a snack, go for a turkey or chicken sandwich. No chips. No weight creep."

Something New Under the Sun

There are five ways to die on the golf course, says the American Academy of Dermatology:

1. Get hit by a golf ball.
2. Get run over by a golf cart.
3. Get whacked by a golf club.
4. Get struck by lightning.
5. Forget your hat.

Now that the AAD has our attention, can we talk? Although the risk of absorbing the rays that cause skin cancer is higher during the summer, it can happen at any time of the year. If we're on the course, we're at risk.

QUICK REVIEW

But there are ways to reduce this risk—some old, some new.

- ✓ Minimize your amount of exposure to the sun between 10 A.M. and 4 P.M. That's when harmful rays are the strongest.

- ✓ Cover up. Wear a hat with a brim (not a straw hat) that's at least 4 inches wide. Wear long sleeves when it's practical.

- ✓ Wear sunglasses that provide 99 percent protection against ultraviolet A and ultraviolet B sunlight.

- ✓ Avoid tanning beds. Enough said.

- ✓ Ask your doctor about medications that can increase your sensitivity to sunlight (thiazide, tetracycline, sulfa antibiotics, ibuprofen).

- ✓ Use a sunscreen with a sun protection factor of at least 15, even on a cloudy day. If you're particularly sensitive to the sun, use a sunscreen of 30 or higher. Whatever the number, apply the substance 20 to 30 minutes before you go out and reapply it periodically (every 30 to 60 minutes if you're sweating).

THE NEW STUFF

A substance called Parsol 1789 is now on the market. It provides maximum protection against UVA rays. Your dermatologist knows about it, but your pharmacist may not. Look for the ingredient "avobenzone" on the label. Ombrelle, Presun Ultra, and Shade UVA Guard are three trade names of products that contain Parsol 1789.

Remember that a suntan means you've been burned. You might like the look now, but wrinkles and age spots (of which we have enough already) are a high price to pay for this look. Skin cancer is the ultimate price.

If you do develop a burn, take this Mayo Clinic advice:

✓ Use aspirin or ibuprofen for pain.

✓ Apply cold compresses.

✓ Stay out of the sun until the burn heals.

Lightning Round

Get ready for a lesson in golf-after-50 safety. If you're on the course and can hear thunder, you're close enough to a storm to be struck by lightning. To figure out how close, use the flash-to-bang formula. Flash-to-bang is the time that elapses between seeing a flash of lightning and hearing the thunder that follows. For each five-second count, lightning is 1 mile away. For example, thunder heard 20 seconds after a flash translates to a distance of 4 miles; 15 seconds, 3 miles; 5 seconds, 1 mile.

When lightning is within 3 miles (and preferably sooner than that), take cover, but not just anywhere. Stay away from tents, golf carts, hilltops, metal bleachers, water, open spaces, and isolated trees. It's okay to seek protection in a forest, because the number of trees in the stand reduces the odds of being hit. On your way to a safer area, temporarily get rid of things like watches, carts, clubs, and cleated shoes.

NOWHERE TO HIDE

If there's no nearby shelter and things are getting scary, find a low spot (such as a ditch) away from trees, fences, and poles. Squat low, but don't sit or lie down. Place your hands on your knees with your head as low as possible. The trick is to make yourself as small as possible and to minimize the amount of contact you have with the ground. You won't be comfortable, but we're talking about surviving to play another day. Stay at least 15 feet away from other people. No group hugs, no group strikes.

When you think it's over, it may not be. It's best to wait a minimum of 30 minutes after the last lightning strike before gathering your belongings and resuming play or returning to the clubhouse.

The Cold War

The average after-50 golfer gets between one and six colds per year, but susceptibility increases with age and with the number of people we're around. Golfers aren't likely to stay off the course because of a cold. Should we? And what effect does exercise have on the severity and duration of cold symptoms?

The second question has been answered by a study conducted at Ball State University. Researchers at the Human Performance Laboratory found that moderate exercise during a typical cold caused by a rhinovirus does not appear to affect the severity of symptoms or the length of a cold. Even exercise at 70 percent of maximum heart rate for 40 minutes on 10 consecutive days—pretty intense for most after-50 exercisers—was not enough to affect the body's immune response one way or another.

IS IT OKAY TO PLAY?

The answer to the "Should we exercise with a cold?" question is based on both science and common sense. If you feel too ill to play golf, don't, for your sake and out of consideration for those you might infect. But it's probably safe for most of us to play when we have minor cold symptoms.

Here are some useful guidelines. If your symptoms are above the neck (runny nose, sneezing, sore throat), it's okay to exercise and to play golf if you can reasonably protect those around you from catching whatever it is you have. You can even increase the intensity of your exercise (walking the course or exercising apart from golf) if your symptoms diminish during the first few minutes of exercise.

WHEN TO STAY AT HOME

However, exercise is not recommended if you have below-the-neck symptoms such as fever, sore muscles, achy joints, vomiting, diarrhea, or a cough that produces mucus. If you're experiencing any of those problems, let the cold run its course before you get back on the course or engage in any other kind of physical activity.

Red Flags in the Sunset

Golfers in general and after-50 golfers in particular are bombarded with information about gadgets, supplements, and products that are supposed to make us stronger, fitter, and healthier. The manufacturers know who we are and where to find us. They do not, to their credit, claim to make us wealthier, and they don't. Before you spend money on any health- or fitness-related product, consider the following red flags.

ENDORSEMENTS

If an ad presents a celebrity golfer or entertainment figure, watch out. We are expected to assume that these people have used the product to improve their health, fitness, or golf game. The testimonial of a single golfer, athlete, or television star means that either he or she was paid to make the ad, or the product worked for that person. Without evidence from controlled studies, testimonials mean nothing. What works for one person, no matter how sincere, may not work for someone else.

SPECIAL EQUIPMENT

If you have to buy special equipment like machines, belts, or other contraptions to get the benefits, back off. For example, hundreds of weight-training devices flood the market every year. None of them has been proven more effective than traditional free weights or machines.

VAGUE CLAIMS

Be skeptical when you hear vague claims of scientific proof. Where was this research conducted? How many people participated in the study? Have other studies confirmed the findings? Was the research funded by the product's manufacturer? Were the subjects in our age group? In other words, give us some substance here, rather than hard-to-prove claims.

LIES

The last red flag is called a lie. And we already know that not all advertisers tell the truth, the whole truth, and nothing but the truth. There may be something to magnets for joint and muscle pain, but the company that claims absolute scientific proof of their effectiveness is lying. The data are simply not there—at least not yet. The product that's supposed to help you lose weight while sleeping, doesn't. Copper bracelets for arthritis pain are not exactly embraced by the Arthritis Foundation. The diet of the month that promises permanent weight loss may be dangerous. Remember phen-phen?

Don't get us wrong. There are some great products on the market that are effective, safe, and worthy of consideration. Vitamin or mineral supplements for those who have deficiencies, sports drinks, basic exercise machines (treadmills, stationary cycles, stair climbers), and heart-rate monitors are examples. And there is, of course, the placebo effect. There is no science to support the use of copper bracelets, for example, but if you *think* they reduce pain or increase range of motion, they probably do.

There is a small but increasing body of evidence supporting the use of therapeutic magnets for reduction of pain. For a limited number of people (but not those using pacemakers or other artificial, internal medical devices), they may work. If and when they do, no one is sure why.

Here's the take-home message: Before you write the check for a questionable health or medical product, check for the red flags.

5 where does it hurt?

This section will help you distinguish between routine pain and dangerous pain, learn how to manage pain, and know which pills to take—as well as which ones not to take—for pain, fever, and inflammation. What can you do about cramps? Is there a chance that orthotics might eliminate or reduce discomfort throughout the body? When and how long should you apply ice to an injured area? Is massage just a "feel good" rub-down or does it have therapeutic value? When you do get hurt, how can you speed up the recovery process to get back on the course as soon as possible? The answers start here.

Predicting
Your Next Injury

Your next golf injury is likely to be either your lower back or your left wrist. While professional golfers usually suffer injuries because they practice too much, you'll probably get hurt because you aren't in good physical condition or have a faulty swing.

LOWER BACK

Injuries to the lower back account for approximately 30 percent of all golf injuries. A strain of the muscles in the lumbar region is the single most frequent complaint. The injury occurs because of the extreme twisting motion golfers use taking the club away, twisting the hips into the shot at impact, and following through.

WHAT TO DO

Stand in a more upright position when you address the ball and reduce the degree of hip rotation. That puts less stress on the back. However, since the rotation of the hips is crucial to generating power, you may have to make a choice: more hip rotation and more power versus less rotation and less distance.

WRIST

Among right-handers, the left wrist is most likely to be injured (24 percent of all golf injuries); only 3 percent of injuries involve the right wrist. In addition to repetitive trauma, contact with thick playing surfaces can contribute to excessive resistance.

WHAT TO DO

Try an exercise called Wrist Rollers. Rolling up a 2- to 3-pound weight suspended on a cord and attached to a handle can add strength to your arms and wrists and help you withstand the forces that cause wrist injuries.

Are You Really Hurt?

After 50, playing with pain may be the norm rather than the exception. Sore muscles, stiff joints, and other parts of the body that don't work as well as they used to are facts of golfing life. If we wait for a day when we feel absolutely pain-free, we may never play again.

ROUTINE PAIN

Routine pain comes from playing a round or two of golf. It hits players of all ages. There are no long-term consequences. Aspirin, ibuprofen, naproxen, ketoprofen, or acetaminophen, plus ice and a good warm-up, can get most of us back to as near normal as we're going to get.

DANGEROUS PAIN

Dangerous pain, on the other hand, is the kind that can cause irreversible damage. "Playing through the pain," "sucking it up," and "no pain, no gain," are attitudes that can get us in a lot of trouble. Our bodies are telling us to back off or pay a long-term price.

So how do we distinguish between routine pain and dangerous pain? Dr. Ben Kibler, an orthopedic surgeon in Lexington, Kentucky, has developed a pain rating scale to help us determine when an injury is severe enough to cut back on golf and get medical attention.

THE PAIN RATINGS AND HOW TO MANAGE THEM

Level 1 pain hurts after you've exercised but goes away by the next day. Treat it with ice, over-the-counter pain medicine, and stretching both before and after exercise.

Level 2 pain develops during a round of golf but doesn't interfere with the way you swing or move. The treatment is the same as for Level 1, but it's best to take it as easy as possible on the course.

Level 3 is pain that continues while you're playing and interferes with your game. Get medical attention and treatment before you play again.

At Level 4, the pain is there even when you aren't exercising, and it severely restricts your ability to play golf or do any physical activity. Get to a sports medicine doctor right now.

Where Are My Pills?

Golfers know about aches, sore muscles, pain, and pain pills. But there's widespread confusion regarding specific effects of over-the-counter pain medications. Some are good for pain, some for inflammation, some for fever, and some for all three. Can you match the pill with its purpose? If not, read on.

ASPIRIN

Aspirin is not only the most effective nonprescription drug for pain, but it can also reduce fever and inflammation. And it's now recommended by many physicians as part of a heart disease prevention program. But aspirin can irritate the lining of the stomach, and it acts as a blood thinner, so it's not for everyone.

ACETAMINOPHEN

Acetaminophen (Tylenol is the most recognized trade name) is great for pain and fever, but does nothing for inflammation. Taken as directed there are no side effects, but overdoses can be deadly.

EVERYTHING ELSE

The remaining three substances on the list below—ibuprofen, naproxen, and ketoprofen—all have the potential for causing stomach problems. Take them with food to reduce that possibility. All but acetaminophen can reduce inflammation, but they may take a few hours or a few days to have an effect. Here is a quick-look checklist to sort out the confusion over the benefits of pain relievers.

A word about ibuprofen, Motrin, and Celebrex. Heavy, long-term use of ibuprofen can be dangerous; digestive irritation and liver malfunctions are possibilities. Check with your doctor on how much is too much. Motrin is 800 milligrams of ibuprofen. Take enough ibuprofen and you are, in essence, taking a prescription drug. Celebrex is a relatively new prescription anti-inflammatory drug that's very effective. It does not cause stomach distress in most people, but others simply cannot tolerate it. Ask your physician if you can try some samples (to see how you react) before committing to a full prescription.

SUBSTANCE	PAIN	FEVER	INFLAMMATION
Aspirin	yes	yes	yes
Acetaminophen	yes	yes	no
Ibuprofen	yes	*	yes
Naproxen	yes	no	yes
Ketoprofen	yes	**	yes

* Not as effective as aspirin and acetaminophen.
** Not frequently recommended for fever.

Are You
Injury-Prone?

Think back over the injuries you've sustained since you turned 50. If you've had more than your share, you may be injury-prone. Don't despair. It happens to people our age. But there are things you can do to cut down on the number of injuries and to enjoy your time on the golf course more.

OVERUSE

Most leg injuries are the result of overuse. You may be playing more frequently than your body can tolerate. It needs time to recover from exercise, even if the exercise is relatively mild. *Solution:* Reduce the total number of rounds over a period of time and allow for some breaks between rounds.

MUSCLE WEAKNESS

Aging causes all of us to lose predictable amounts of strength unless we do something about it. *Solution:* Start a light strength-training program for your calf muscles. Simply standing with your toes and forefoot on a step and lifting your body weight is a good start.

LACK OF FLEXIBILITY

The less flexible we become, the more likely we are to strain a muscle. *Solution:* About two minutes of stretching exercises every day or before every round. Stand 2 to 3 feet away from a wall, keep both feet flat on the floor, and use both hands to support your body weight while leaning forward. Three 10-second repetitions or one 30-second rep ought to be enough. Don't stretch to the point that it hurts.

TOO MUCH, TOO SOON

When some of us finally get free time to play a lot of golf, we overdo it. *Solution:* The rule that serious athletes follow is never to increase the intensity of exercise by more than 10 percent a week. You can do the math, but measure it on the golf course by days played, rounds, distance walked, or time.

FOOD AND DRINK

Yes, what goes into a 50-plus body can show up in faraway places like the feet, ankles, legs, and knees. Cramps, pulled muscles, sore tendons, and aching joints can be related to diet. *Solution:* Monitor your intake of calories, carbohydrates, protein, and calcium. Try to make the connection between food and injuries. If you can't, ask a sports nutritionist for help.

Unsolved Mysteries: Muscle Cramps

As common as muscle cramps are, no one knows for sure what causes them. What we do know is that certain muscles, under circumstances that vary from person to person, involuntarily contract. When they do, no one has to tell you what's happening. The symptom is sudden, excruciating, unforgettable pain.

DEHYDRATION?

The theories on causes of muscle cramps are almost as numerous as the number of muscles that can be affected. One explanation is that cramps are caused by dehydration. Golfers, among others, get cramps when they don't replace the fluid they're losing through sweat. Avoid cramps, we're told, by drinking fluids that don't contain alcohol or caffeine before, during, and after a round of golf. Nice theory and good advice, but there's little research that makes a direct connection between fluid loss and cramps.

ELECTROLYTE IMBALANCE?

The second theory on the great muscle cramp mystery is "electrolyte imbalance," a technical way to say that we need certain minerals to maintain body processes. What are those minerals? Chloride, potassium, and sodium, for starters. Lose too much sodium and its balance with potassium is affected. Lose too much potassium—which is hard to do—and an imbalance in the opposite direction occurs. Either way, the lack of potassium could lead to muscle cramps— maybe. So take in enough sodium (about 2,400 milligrams a day) and eat foods like fruits and vegetables. Might help; can't hurt.

HOT AND HUMID?

Theory number three guesses that extreme weather conditions, like extremely hot and extremely humid, make the electrolyte imbalance already mentioned more likely to happen. There are lots of locker room stories supporting this theory, but no real proof. You can make the same argument about lack of training, but weekend golfers get cramps, as do world-class athletes.

FATIGUE?

Some relatively new evidence suggests that cramps are (1) associated with electrical activity that (2) leads to muscle fatigue that (3) causes cramps. New to scientists, but not new to athletes and trainers. They noticed the fatigue factor a long time ago. That a stretching program can both prevent and treat cramps can't be proven in the lab, but it makes sense.

YOU SOLVE THE MYSTERY

This is one mystery you may have to solve by yourself. There's probably some validity to each of the muscle cramp theories. And you can't go wrong by drinking fluids, eating a well-balanced diet, avoiding extreme weather conditions, and stretching before and after a round of golf. Those precautions might, at least, reduce the chance of getting cramps. But they don't come with a guarantee.

Need a Lift?

"Heel pain is a common complaint among golfers over the age of 50, but it's not the only one that affects the feet," says Dr. Stephen Pribut, a sports podiatrist who practices in Washington, D.C.

"I see golfers with Morton's neuroma (an enlarged, inflamed nerve), heel spurs, injuries to the small bones of the feet, tendinitis,

and even back pain," adds Pribut, who is on the faculty of the George Washington University School of Medicine.

ORTHOTICS

One treatment suggested by Pribut and other sports medicine specialists is an orthotic, a shoe insert designed to give support or relieve pressure on various parts of the feet. Orthotics allow the feet to hit the ground in a sound mechanical position and allow for a normal rolling-inward motion. They also help the feet get back to a neutral position after they flatten on impact with the ground.

How do you know if you need the orthotics that can be bought at a drugstore or the prescription kind? One tip-off is recurring injuries. If your condition improves with a store-bought insert, then gets worse, or if a secondary injury develops, get help from an orthopedic surgeon or a podiatrist. Over-the-counter orthotics are more like arch supports. They can be useful in easing mild conditions and are less expensive than prescription inserts.

GET HELP

Pribut warns that each foot moves differently during a golf swing. The back foot must allow for more pronation during the follow-through than the front foot. That's another reason for seeing a professional to get an initial evaluation of a foot problem.

Orthotics can temporarily correct a problem, or they can be used indefinitely. Many athletes, including golfers over 50, use them forever because they can walk and run more efficiently and comfortably. If you're having lower-extremity pain, consider the orthotics alternative.

The Ice Age

The next time you stop by the 19th hole for something cool to drink, think twice about what to do with the ice. Instead of ordering it in your drink, you'd probably feel better if you put it on your shoulder. Wouldn't hurt to use it both ways.

If 99 percent of all baseball pitchers in the big leagues ice down their shoulders after throwing 100 or so pitches, why shouldn't those of us in the after-50 group do the same thing after 70-plus golf swings during a round? And that's not counting the warm-up and practice swings.

REDUCE SWELLING AND SORENESS

"The consensus among trainers in all sports," explains Dr. Gene Coleman, strength and conditioning coach for the Houston Astros, "is that repetitive motion produces microtrauma in the muscles that are being utilized. In golf, tennis, and baseball, that means the arm and shoulder. Ice applied for even 10 minutes after a game or round inhibits potential swelling and reduces the soreness that can develop immediately or the next day."

How you apply the ice is less important than simply doing the deed. Most trainers place ice packs over a T-shirt or towel and hold them in place with an elastic bandage. You can rig up something similar in the clubhouse or at home. Inexpensive and reusable chemical packs achieve the same effect. Don't place either directly on the skin.

A particularly sore arm or shoulder responds even better to an ice massage, according to a study reported in the *Journal of Orthopedic and Sports Physical Therapy.* Fill some paper cups with water, freeze them, then apply the ice directly to the sore muscle by gradually tearing the paper away as the ice melts. Constantly moving the ice should prevent skin damage, but be careful.

WHAT TO DO

Give ice a shot if you tend to get sore after a round. At our age, anything that reduces muscle stiffness and gets us ready for the next 18 holes is worth a try. You may have to endure a few snickers, but you have nothing to lose but a few ice cubes.

Rubbing It In

By the age of 50 most golfers have had the fortune—or misfortune, depending on their point of view—of experiencing a wide range of treatments for golf injuries. But have you considered a sports massage?

"The majority of my clients are recreational golfers who play at least twice a week," says Annette Helm, a Scarsdale, New York, massage therapist. "Massage is beneficial for lots of reasons, but the most important one is circulation. If a muscle is stiff because of a long day on the course, getting oxygenated blood to the area improves the condition rapidly."

BEFORE A ROUND

Helm adds that there are also reasons to get a massage before a round of golf. "Massage makes the muscles more pliable and may lessen the chance of injury. The pre-exercise massage is a little different from the one you would get after playing. It's designed to provide more of an energizing feel."

Even exercise scientists who are skeptical about the benefits of massage—and there are plenty of them—admit that manipulating soft tissues feels good. No one knows exactly why. Maybe there are physiological explanations, or perhaps the reasons are more psychological than physical. It doesn't matter. If feeling good or feeling better than you felt before a massage is your objective, a massage will help you achieve that goal. *The Physician and Sportsmedicine,* a respected journal of medical information, says, "Massage can give an athlete a psychological boost. And often, that psychological factor is the component that makes a champion."

A PERFORMANCE CONNECTION?

However, connecting massage and performance is hard to do. One professional journal says there's no evidence that massage has any positive effects on the ability to perform or on the long-term rate of muscle recovery. Another says that it does not speed up the removal of blood lactate, a claim often made by therapists.

What we do know is that therapeutic massage increases circulation, "loosens up" muscles, reduces pain and swelling, and decreases blood pressure and heart rate. For most of us, that's enough.

Returning to Action

"Neither snow nor rain nor heat nor gloom of night stays these couriers (and after-50 golfers) from the completion of their appointed rounds."

But eagerness to complete a round of golf following an injury or illness is risky. Getting back on the course before our bodies are ready is a sure way to put us back into rehab or on the couch, instead of out there where we really belong.

All of us would like to know exactly how long it will take before we can play golf again after getting hurt, and most of us don't want wait as long as we should. For most injuries, there are general time-required guidelines, but there are too many individual differences to make precise predictions.

ANSWER THESE QUESTIONS

More important than a specific time frame needed for recovery, you, your doctor, and your physical therapist (if you have one) need answers to the following 10 questions offered by the *Gatorade Sports Science Exchange*. With this information, you'll know whether or not you're ready to rejoin your foursome.

1. Are you still in pain, or can you play with the pain that remains?

2. If you play golf, will the injured area remain free of swelling?

3. Are you in the latter stages of a rehabilitation program that a doctor has prescribed?

4. Do you have enough range of motion to play golf without re-injuring yourself?

5. Has someone (other than your spouse, who is probably eager to get you out of the house) signed off on your strength, power, endurance, and general fitness to play golf?

6. Do you have braces, pads, tape, or any other kind of equipment that will prevent further injury?

7. Are you informed enough to recognize the potential for re-injury when it exists?

8. Are you willing to continue an exercise program, if recommended, after you resume play?

9. Are you injury-prone or re-injury-prone, and is there anything you can do about it?

10. Are you ready to play golf without the fear of getting hurt again?

The more times you can answer yes to these ten questions, the more prepared you are to return to action. There are ways to speed up the recovery process. Read about them in "Get Well Soon."

Get Well Soon

Most after-50 golfers are used to the fact that when we wake up every morning, something is probably going to hurt. That doesn't mean we have to like it, and it doesn't mean we can't do something about it. Within reasonable limits, there are ways to speed up the recovery process and get back onto the golf course.

ICE IT

If the injury involves muscles or joints, put ice on it immediately. Even before you call a physician, use ice applications to limit swelling and inflammation. Don't wait until the round is over and don't wait until you get home. Use ice off and on for at least the first 48 hours, and perhaps beyond. After that, heat is okay to relieve soreness and for warming up, but it's not very effective for healing.

DIAGNOSE IT

The next step, assuming the injury is serious enough, is to get an accurate diagnosis. You can't speed up anything until you know exactly what you're dealing with. Instead of letting something rock along, hoping it'll get better, get to a sports medicine physician, trainer, or physical therapist. But know your insurance coverage.

Does it allow you to bypass the family physician and go straight to a specialist? These professionals see sports injuries every day, as opposed to the general practitioners who see similar problems occasionally.

MEDICATE IT

If anti-inflammatory medicine has been prescribed, take it exactly as prescribed for the entire amount of time recommended by your doctor. Don't stop when the symptoms subside. And don't take someone else's medicine. Just because it worked for another person doesn't mean it will be effective or safe for you.

EXERCISE IT

As soon as the symptoms subside or when you get clearance from a doctor, start limited range-of-motion exercises. Once you can do that, add very mild strengthening exercises. Because the muscles automatically shut down after an injury, it's important to reverse the muscle atrophy (wasting away) process as soon as possible.

THEN ASK YOURSELF . . .

Finally, go back and ask yourself the questions in "Returning to Action." If you pass that test, you should be ready to play sooner than your friends who don't follow the get-well-soon rules.

6 the back nine

Enough, already, about strokes, strength, suggestions, senior health, and sore muscles. It's time to lighten up and hear about the experiences that make our game especially enjoyable. Find out what Turkey's Rules of Golf are, then read the avalanche of e-mails our Web site received from around the country with Turkey Helper —variations on Turkey's original rules.

Are after-50 golfers superstitious? No. *Superstitious* is a word that is not strong enough to describe the extreme behavior many of us exhibit before, during, and after a round of golf. We have taken superstition to the level of science.

What goes on in golfers' heads? You probably don't want to know everything, but mental conditions like the yips, poor preparation, lack of concentration, and a strong case of the jitters are as curable as they are real.

Turkey's Rules of Golf

There are The Rules of Golf, the bend-but-don't-break rules that many senior players observe, and then there are Turkey Righter's Rules.

Turkey, of Bedford, New York, is 97 and actually shot his age and better when he was 92. He observes every rule of golf etiquette, never moving while another is hitting, never walking in the line of someone's putt, and never hitting out of turn, though he admittedly gets more than his share of turns because he is not long off the tee.

However, Turkey's Rules of Golf are not consistent with The Rules of Golf. Face it, when you've survived—no, thrived—for nearly 100 years, you have a right to play Turkey's Rules of Enjoyment. Here are a few:

- ✓ When you hit a ball into a trap and prefer not to play it out of the trap, place the ball to the side of the trap. Makes a lot of sense.

- ✓ If you think your shot went into the fairway but can't see it or find it, a gopher hole was clearly the culprit. Just place the ball where you think it probably went. If you can't see it, the problem doesn't exist.

- ✓ Never hit a ball out of very high grass. You might injure yourself, and it's unfair. Move the ball to shorter grass and proceed.

✓ Never charge yourself for a lost ball. If it's headed for water, drop where you think it stopped and take your next shot. Don't ask. Don't tell.

At a certain point in life, when the body just won't respond, it's right to bend the rules, and Turkey reached that point long ago. *A Different Game: Golf After 50* celebrates Turkey Righter, his rules, and all of those super seniors who still get out there and have fun.

Turkey Helper

The response to our original Turkey's Rules column was enthusiastic. Not only did Web site readers like his ideas about how the game should be played after the age of 50 (or, in Turkey's case, 90), but many of them also responded with their own Turkey's Rules of Golf. So here are some more of Turkey's Rules—"Turkey Helper," we'll call them.

- ✓ Play must be continuous—dead slow. Perhaps not the best choice of words, but you get the message.

- ✓ The ball is in an unrepaired, half-repaired, or sand-filled divot: Bad luck. Pros don't have to put up with these conditions. Neither should we. Move it.

- ✓ Two-stroke penalty if a player uses a club with a cost exceeding $200.

- ✓ No 4-putts. Three is the limit. Also, no score over 5 shall be entered on a scorecard.

- ✓ It is impolite to hit while someone is talking. Wait until he or she finishes the story, then hit.

- ✓ On a really bad hole, there is no need to count every shot. Just estimate what you should have scored.

✓ Always play "Ready Golf." Never wait around for others in your group to hit. Play when you're ready, as long as you don't hit into the group ahead of yours.

✓ Restricted swings or restricted lines of flight are prohibited. If something is in the way, move your ball to an unrestricted area.

✓ Do not hit a ball off rocks or roots. You could damage a club or injure yourself.

✓ After hitting an errant shot, turn to your foursome and say, "I'm sorry, I didn't intend to hit that shot, so I'll take another." If you say all of this before the ball hits the ground, you may do so with no penalty.

The Science of Superstition

We may not be more superstitious than younger golfers, but we've had more time to contemplate and refine our beliefs. By now our superstitions have endured and moved toward science. No matter how ridiculous, we are firm in our superstitions and we're sticking to them. So here's a starter list of golf superstitions submitted by readers who were given advance notice.

"Don't talk to my ball. After I strike the ball on a putt, be quiet. If I miss the shot, it's because your comments affected the path of the ball. I'm serious."

—Jes, Louisiana

"If I'm playing well, whatever I'm wearing stays on the entire round. It doesn't matter if it was 40 degrees when I started the round and now it's 83, I'm wearing long-sleeved shirts, sweaters, jackets, the whole deal. Of course, if I start playing badly, I'll dress more reasonably."

—Mike, Ohio

"I never buy a golf ball, period. It's not that I'm cheap. I'm retired and have no money worries. But I can't play with a ball other than one that I find. I figure if it's been lost, it's looking for a new owner.

When I find it, I know that it wanted to be mine and for a reason that has to be good."

—Jim, Massachusetts

Finally, Australian golfer Adam Holden offers this four-pack:

- ✓ On a trip to the United States, he packs 300 Day-Glo orange tees. "Won't use anything but, mate."

- ✓ "If I change spikes on my shoes, each spike must be exactly the same. No mix-and-match jobs. And I change them a lot, because if one is worn just a bit, out they all come."

- ✓ "If someone touches my clubs prior to a tournament, I'm ready to see a psychiatrist or withdraw or fight because I figure I've just lost all chance of winning or playing well."

- ✓ "I eat a ham sandwich before each tournament and it *must* be between two pieces of bread. It cannot be on any kind of bread roll."

From Office to Tee

"How often do you rush from your home or office to the course to make your tee time?" asks Dr. Evan Brody, a sports psychophysiologist and president of Performance Enhancement Consultants in Olney, Maryland. "Do you catch yourself working on mechanics as you warm up on the practice tee? Does it take a few holes to discover your golf game?"

A WHAT?

Let's back up for a moment. A sports psychophysiologist? Well, yes. Brody combines his background and training in education, exercise science, psychology, and even martial arts into what amounts to a new discipline, or at least an innovative approach to an old one. Traditional sports psychology works mostly with the mind. Brody takes that concept to the course and teaches people, through a series of drills, how to connect the mind to the physical demands of playing golf.

A scratch golfer named Bob told Brody that he turns off thoughts about the office and begins his mental preparation for an upcoming round "as soon as my office door hits me in the behind." Bob does not carry a cell phone. On the way to the course, he devotes his thoughts to what he wants to accomplish for his game that day and how he's going to execute his game plan.

"Once you arrive at the course or club," adds Brody, who has worked with PGA, LPGA, and Senior PGA Tour players, "preparation should consist of warming up your body and preparing your mind to allow your body to carry out the plan. During the warm-up, focus on the feel of your swing rather than all the smaller mechanical parts. You might even try what some tour players do by hitting a few balls with your eyes closed. Relax, focus, and trust your swing." (Better try that one at home first.)

MANAGE YOUR TIME

Brody's message, which has barely been introduced here, is to manage your time on and off the course. "Take a little time to mentally and physically prepare before you get to the first tee. Not only will it lead to a better round of golf, it may save you from wrapping that driver around the next tree."

First Impressions

Sometimes after-50 golfers think too much. How many times do you read a green, line up to make a putt, then back off for a second look? You think you have a better line for the putt but when you get back over the ball, you hesitate, indecisive.

"Hesitation due to indecision will interfere with muscular coordination and control, resulting in a less-than-satisfactory putt," warns Dr. Evan Brody. "Indecisiveness comes mostly from lack of confidence and lack of confidence comes from not playing well lately."

How are we supposed to get through those periods of indecision and back to a more comfortable and confident game? "Make a commitment!" says Brody. "Commit to your first thought, your first instinct, and, in this case, your first read. Even if you're wrong, it's better to be committed to a shot than to suffer from the hesitation that results when you can't make a decision."

TRY THIS EXPERIMENT

Brody suggests the following exercise to learn how to trust first instincts. For two weeks, trust your first thought, hit the putt, and document the results of the decision. During the next two weeks, do the same thing every time you back up, take another look, and go with your second look. Compare the results.

"Similar to taking an exam," explains Brody, "you'll find that your first thought is usually correct. Once you prove to yourself that your first decisions are worthy of your trust, you'll be on the road to recovery. If not, call me."

Beating the Yips

Sports psychologists refer to it as "performance-related anxiety" or an "involuntary motor disturbance." Golfers call it the "yips"—the inability to calmly, deliberately, and smoothly stroke a putt.

THE SYMPTOMS

Whatever "it" is called, a golfer with the yips feels that the muscles are tightening up. "Some people can't pull the trigger on a 6-foot putt," says Dr. Robert Rotella, director of sports psychology at the University of Virginia. "They start doubting themselves. When they finally do putt, they 'muscle' the ball instead of stroking it. Others have a spastic feeling when they move the club head. Their motion is jerky, as if they have tremors in their arms or hands.

"Everybody wants to blame the yips on nerve damage or age," continues Rotella, "but the truth is that yips develop because some golfers put too much pressure on themselves. They might worry about what their friends will think if they miss. If these golfers had a serious neurological problem, it would show up in every part of their game."

HAVE A PLAN

Have a plan if a case of the yips surfaces. Refocus. Mentally rehearse before you go out to play. Develop a pre-putt routine. Take a deep breath. Change putters. Return to fundamentally sound golf. Visualize a realistic margin of error. Think the same way on every putt. These are some of ways in which after-50 golfers nip the yips.

Concentration
Lost and Found

"Mindfulness is the solution to poor concentration," says Roanoke, Virginia, sports psychologist Dr. John Heil. "The idea is to have a mind full of what you are doing at the moment."

After-50 golfers, like children playing a game, have to become completely absorbed in the task. For the moment, the goal is to

reach a frame of mind in which the thoughts that distract most adults don't even exist.

PLAY A LOT OF GOLF

How do you get there? The first way is by playing golf as much as is reasonable. It's hard to simply turn the concentration switch on and off at will. The more you're in competitive situations, the better your concentration skills become. Better concentration breeds confidence, and confidence removes self-doubt. Both come with playing time.

PRACTICE MENTAL SKILLS

The second path to concentration is by practicing mental skills. You don't have to get too cerebral here, but there's something to be said for imagining yourself in pressure situations even if you're just playing a practice round. Then you'll have the benefit of virtual experience during tournament competition.

WHAT HAPPENS WHEN YOU LOSE IT?

Just because golfers learn to block out distractions and focus on the moment, that doesn't mean they can concentrate for extended periods of time. In fact, it's unrealistic. One technique for regaining concentration is to return to the basics of executing skills. Instead of trying to make up for a mistake caused by poor concentration, make the best possible decision about what to do next.

Play the ball, not the opponent, the course, or the score. Think about what you want to do, not what might go wrong. If you're going to worry, worry about things you can correct and let go of everything else.

Heil has a three-part plan for refocusing when you become distracted:

1. Stop what you're doing and will yourself into not thinking about other things. If you have to talk to yourself, do it.

2. Take a deep breath and compose yourself. Call a 20-second time-out.

3. Focus on a "performance cue" such as the ball, your swing, or a target. Ignore the bigger picture.

"By removing distractions," concludes Heil, "you're training yourself to think less. The ultimate goal is for technique, intensity, and focus to happen unconsciously. If you have to think about it, you haven't reached that goal. But keep working on it."

Nervous Is Normal

One of the great myths of professional golf is that elite players don't get nervous. Let's make it official. They do. Hale Irwin gets nervous. Tom Watson gets nervous. Tiger Woods gets nervous.

The difference between these great players and some of us is that they've learned how to manage their nerves in ways that don't run their scores up. Some of them even use what sports psychologists call "performance anxiety" to get an advantage over their opponents.

According to Dr. Shane Murphy, author of *The Achievement Zone*, many golfers either avoid stressful competition or panic when they're in the middle of it. The ones who pass on tournament competition tend to be good on the practice tee and in low-pressure situations, but terrible when their play counts for something more. Others compete, but not as well as they could if they worked on managing their emotions.

SIX WAYS TO RELAX

There are at least six ways to relax under pressure. Although all are more complex than we have room to describe in detail, here are Murphy's basic strategies:

1. Take regular, deep breaths during a round and before a shot when you feel a case of the jitters coming on.

2. Try relaxing your muscles by contracting them, then exhaling and letting them go back to normal.

3. When you get nervous, stop or at least change the pace of your play, refocus, and calm down.

4. Get a mental picture of how you want to swing the club on your next shot.

5. Practice getting your body to respond to suggestions or cues you give it *(swing through the ball; take a controlled backswing; rotate the shoulders).*

6. Talk yourself through situations on the course. Be positive and confident.

Murphy's message for after-50 golfers is to expect to get nervous at times. It's normal behavior. Select one or more of the relaxation strategies listed above and practice them. You'll find that your nervousness can be channeled into productive energy and sharpened concentration when you need them the most.

Any final words? No. After 50, golf *is* a different game, but it's fun to just keep rolling the ball in the direction of the hole.

index